Reflecting Jesus in the City
CHRISTLIKE MINISTRY IN URBAN IMMIGRANT CONTEXTS

John D. Trotter

Endorsements

Drawing from his rich experience in immigrant communities and his rooting in Scripture, John Trotter has written a book that is filled with practical wisdom, honest reflection, and prayerful insight. By focusing on the character and practices of Jesus and on how they can shape life, ministry, and mission in urban America, Trotter offers a fresh and welcome way of approaching the challenges and blessings of following Jesus in the city. This book is the good fruit of one who has lived the material he addresses.

Christine D. Pohl
Professor of Christian Ethics, Asbury Theological Seminary
Author of *Making Room: Recovering Hospitality as a Christian Tradition*

John Trotter's new title *Reflecting Jesus in the City: Christlike Ministry in Urban Immigrant Contexts* is an excellent new contribution to the field of "diaspora missiology."

The author's passion for ministry in urban context and his professional expertise came through. I am privileged to preview the pre-publication manuscript and my experience in reading it has been both easy (in terms of style and lack of technical jargon) and hard (the challenge of its content) at the same time.

Practitioners will enjoy the author's insights and researchers will be inspired by the message of this book.

Enoch Wan
Research Professor and Director of Doctor of Intercultural
Studies Program, Western Seminary
Founder/Editor, globalmissiology.net and Former President of
Evangelical Missiological Society

How can a blind man have bifocal vision?! John Trotter with his visual impairment shows us: zooming in on the one hand into the life of Jesus in its first century context and then zooming out on the other hand into the lives of Asian immigrants to 21st century USA. Trotter's work with Bhutanese-Nepali refugees means that his bifocality extends to the ends of the earth, even, so that those of us Americans who have a heart for the city and the mission of God can better see (pun intended!) not only how to reflect Jesus' image in the urban spaces within which we currently live and work but also to do so in ways that may have an impact, in our ever-increasingly shrinking global village, on the other side of the world as well. That the Holy Spirit can call and empower every follower of Jesus onto mission, no matter what the obstacle or impairment, is evidenced in this book.

Amos Yong
Director of the Center for Missiological Research and Professor of Theology and Mission, Fuller Theological Seminary
Author of *The Church: A New Vision of the People of God*

John Trotter, in *Reflecting Jesus in the City*, calls us to reflect carefully on important characteristics of Christ's image as we do ministry in urban immigrant communities. He doesn't give the reader easy answers, but rather provides, in each chapter, some tough questions about both our ministry approach and the context in which we operate which are meant to lead to deep reflection and evaluation. The book skillfully provides a very helpful case study from the author's own experiences of urban ministry both in the U.S. and Asia with immigrants and refugees from Bhutan, Nepal and Myanmar. Yet, the author does not provide formulaic approaches or advocate for any specific ministry model. Rather, the book calls the reader to carefully, within the context of ministering together in a team, to ask whether the approaches they are using truly reflect the image of Christ as they seek to live out the Gospel in community. As one who continues to wrestle with doing wholistic and Christ-centered ministry within immigrant communities, and especially amongst newly arriving refugee families, I highly recommend this book because it has made me think, afresh, of what does it mean to walk with and amongst those we serve as we seek to reflect the image of Christ.

Robert Oehrig
Executive Director, Arrive Ministries (World Relief Minnesota)

When migrants, also referred to as diaspora people, cluster in large scale, they give birth to Mega Cities, pluralistic and multicultural societies. John Trotter gives us a "GPS" for migrant ministries to ensure that we can find our way in increasingly culturally complex ministry contexts.

This book is anchored in solid biblical and theological foundations. Its moorings are strongly tied to Christ's missions and ministry models among the "people on the move." The author employs a case study of Bhutanese-Nepali diaspora and immigrants in the USA, but the ministry models are transferable to other diaspora and migrants in all metropolitan areas. This book is a welcome addition to the growing body of diaspora missiology literature. I gladly recommend Trotter's volume to both researchers and practitioners.

Sadiri Joy Tira, DMin, DMiss
Catalyst for Diasporas, The Lausanne Movement

Reflecting Jesus in the City is rich with both theological insights and dozens of practical examples from years of urban ministry, particularly among refugees and other immigrants. It's a super resource for those seeking to minister holistically in urban contexts.

Matthew Soerens
US Director of Church Mobilization, World Relief
Coauthor, *Welcoming the Stranger and Seeking Refuge*

John Trotter is clear -- whatever we are up to in the city, we are not the Messiah sent to save our city, but God's people, reflecting Jesus in our context. He fleshes this out according to various themes in the life of Jesus, each one giving us a rich lens in how the life of Jesus can be reflected in our cities. John wonderfully weaves the stories of Jesus with immigrant stories from our cities and takes us far deeper in what it means to follow and reflect our Lord.

Jude Tiersma Watson
Associate Professor of Urban Mission, Fuller Theological Seminary
Co-Editor of *God So Loves the City* and Co-Leader of
InnerCHANGE Los Angeles

If you are contemplating ministry or engaging in the inner city, this collection of reflections, prayers, poetry, and thoughts is especially for you. John authentically invites us to find and reflect God as we serve, learn, and abide in the city.

Dina González-Piña, MA
Ethnic and Gender Equity Specialist, MCC (Mennonite Central
Committee) and Board Member, CCDA

John Trotter wrote a book for those seeking to do ministry in the new America--one full of immigrants and refugees, people of color and a multitude of faiths and backgrounds. The stories Trotter tells are ones that are familiar to me, as is his premise: Jesus is found in these shifting, changing, glorious and troubled cities. The Holy Spirit is on the move in the forgotten apartment complexes struggling to survive in a culture built around inequality. Are we willing to listen? This book explores communities that are not often profiled (or invited to speak at Christian conferences), and it is a profound and vital and challenging word to slow down and listen to the people that God is using to bring his kingdom into the world.

D.L. Mayfield
Author of *Assimilate or Go Home: Notes from a Failed
Missionary on Rediscovering Faith*

Urban Loft Publishers
P.O. Box 6
Skyforest, CA 92385
www.urbanloftpublishers.com

Senior Editors: Stephen Burris & Kendi Howells Douglas
Copy Editor: Marla Black
Graphics: Elisabeth Arnold

ISBN-13: 978-0-9989177-3-3

Made in the U.S.

To my mom, Jean Trotter - your passion for the presence and glory of Jesus taught me to reflect Him more than anyone I know. May your legacy inspire everyone this book touches.

Series Preface

Urban Mission in the 21st Century is a series of monographs that addresses key issues facing those involved in urban ministry whether it be in the slums, squatter communities, *favelas*, or in immigrant neighborhoods. It is our goal to bring fresh ideas, a theological basis, and best practices in urban mission as we reflect on our changing urban world. The contributors to this series bring a wide-range of ideas, experiences, education, international perspectives, and insight into the study of the growing field of urban ministry. These contributions fall into four very general areas: 1––the biblical and theological basis for urban ministry; 2––best practices currently in use and anticipated in the future by urban scholar/activists who are living working and studying in the context of cities; 3––personal experiences and observations based on urban ministry as it is currently being practiced; and 4––a forward view toward where we are headed in the decades ahead in the expanding and developing field of urban mission. This series is intended for educators, graduate students, theologians, pastors, and serious students of urban ministry.

More than anything, these contributions are creative attempts to help Christians strategically and creatively think about how we can better reach our world that is now more urban than rural. We do not see theology and practice as separate and distinct. Rather, we see sound practice growing out of a healthy vibrant theology that seeks to understand God's world as it truly is as we move further into the twenty-first century. Contributors interact with the best scholarly literature available at the time of writing while making application to specific contexts in which they live and work.

Each book in the series is intended to be a thought-provoking work that represents the author's experience and perspective on urban ministry in a particular context. The editors have chosen those who bring this rich diversity of perspectives to this series. It is our hope and prayer that each book in this series will challenge, enrich, provoke, and cause the reader to dig deeper into subjects that bring the reader to a deeper understanding of our urban world and the ministry the church is called to perform in that new world.

Kendi Howells Douglas and Stephen Burris,
Urban Mission in the 21st Century Series Co-Editors

Table of Contents

Introduction

It's 9:00 p.m., and there's a knock at the door. As Hari burst into our house, I can tell by the look on his face that he didn't just come by to have a cup of tea. Some days these unannounced visits from neighbors bring devastating news where conventional wisdom finds no answer. Other days, the living room is comical with roars of laughter, the sound of a guitar, or the buzz of great stories bouncing off the walls. Ministry life in the city brings the full spectrum of emotions, taking us to places in our hearts we never knew existed. On Monday, we're full of the passion and hope of Christ. By the end of the week, we can often find ourselves exhausted and ready to throw in the towel. Welcome to imitating the life of our Lord. Welcome to *Reflecting Jesus in the City*.

Let's be honest . . . most of us don't believe the city is a very good place. Well, maybe you do because you just picked up this book, but for most in our world, the city is a place to be tolerated at best and a place of total avoidance at the worst. It is somewhat cool for a while, a fun place to visit to expand our perspectives a bit, but who really wants to live there? I can't make any declarations on who does or doesn't want to live in urban centers, but when I look around my neighborhood, there sure are a lot of people here.

If most of the world lives in cities and God loves the world, we have to figure out what it means to reflect Jesus there. We are not called to leave, to retreat, or to fear. We are called to reflect Christ's image to the world evidenced by love for his urban village. Much of the world has come to the gates of American cities, and we want to walk and dwell among its people just as Christ modeled. Understanding the tremendous opportunity and holy privilege before us, we long to demonstrate and announce his beautiful Kingdom in the heart of the city in order that the glory of God be visible to our neighbors. Jesus stepped into neighborhoods in and around Jerusalem and showed his disciples how to live. Through the life of Christ, we learn what it means to be salt and light, to bear truth and hope.

Foundations for Reflecting Jesus in the City

John 1 has become a foundational chapter in understanding the incarnation of Jesus: Immanuel God coming to earth as a man. "The Word became flesh and made his dwelling among us" (John 1:14a). Eugene Peterson's translation in the Message reads, "The Word became flesh and blood, and moved into the neighborhood." Philippians 2:5-8 settles that Jesus did not consider equality with God something to be grasped, but he made himself nothing, taking on the very nature of a servant. Jesus showed us in every way an example in walking with his neighbors amidst some of the most challenging days in history. He preached, he taught, he laughed, he ate, he suffered, he died, he rose. We would all do well, regardless of our context, to take a closer look at how Jesus modeled such a life.

Jesus identified with us, showed us the way of the Kingdom, and gave up his rights in order that we would have new life. In meeting with his disciples upon his resurrection, Jesus empowered his followers through the Spirit commissioning them by saying, "As the Father has sent me, I am sending you" (John 20:21b). God did not give us a motto or website, a building or program when he announced his Kingdom. God sent someone wrapped in flesh and blood. He sent his Son. Jesus moved into the neighborhood and made his dwelling among us. The city needs the person of Jesus to be revealed in love and power.

Though historical social-cultural analysis and urban ministry strategies fill the pages of the chapters ahead, the book is not mostly about that. This book is about Jesus. My heart's single desire is for us all to see Jesus afresh. How did he live? How did he die? What did he call us to?

What I have written here too is also about the city. Namely, it is about my friends and neighbors who have landed in the city after some pretty terrible circumstances. Refugee uprootedness, loss, disability—some tough stuff has landed people here. And then there are others who have chosen, at their own will, to relocate and be part of an urban neighborhood. Urban missionaries, ministry leaders, folks who never left when things got bad—regardless of the label, this book is about them. I have done everything possible to reflect their story accurately and hopefully invite you into a piece of their world that will motivate you to be more like the Jesus urban folks have come to know.

Incarnational Mission Imperfections

In the last fifteen years or so, the word "incarnational" has become a buzzword for anyone who is doing mission that is off the traditional path. The phrase "incarnational ministry" can mean anything from living amongst those you serve, de-emphasizing a church building and focusing on relationships, simply a generic term for urban workers in the slums, or a variety of other mission activities. To be fair, most people are probably envisioning Christ-followers living in close proximity to those they are serving in their neighborhoods, entering into the lives of those around them, and trying to lead them to Jesus. But it seems like over time this term has become excess baggage to urban mission with debates springing up about whether or not it is a good model to use. There was only one Savior and only one incarnation. Is it really the ultimate goal to live as Jesus lived? What about preaching his name, making disciples, or accepting the limitations that we clearly are not the Messiah? Throughout the book, I keep pulling us back to this point. We are not Jesus. We cannot incarnate the Word of God. We can, however, reflect Jesus in the city. Let us try to accept the limitations of the incarnational model and put the centering focus on Christlikeness—his message, his mission, and his life.

No doubt we have all heard comments about what is or what isn't incarnational mission in urban work. Many have gone before me and written invaluable critiques on the topic as well as provided some excellent steps forward in incarnational urban ministry.[1] Let's all admit up front that imperfections abound. May we also acknowledge that we were created in the image of God (Gen. 1:27). From creation until now, our task has been to reflect God's glory to the ends of the earth. *Reflecting Jesus in the City* is my contribution to that task.

---

1. Ross Langmead's seminal work *Word Made Flesh* spells out well the theoretical and practical aspects of incarnational mission. Lingenfelter in *Ministering Cross-Culturally* and Tiersma Watson in her writing on incarnation in *God So Loves the City* have blazed the trail on the topic.

I have chosen to expound on the character traits of Jesus in understanding Christlike ministry in urban contexts because I feel like this is the crux of reflecting his image. The ten postures of Christ addressed are as follows: reflecting his image in mission, in prayer and rest, in suffering, in discipleship, in compassion, in humility, in family, in justice, in community, and in unity. Undoubtedly, we will make decisions about where to live, where to send our kids to school, or what kind of church to plant. That, however, cannot be our starting point. My hope in addressing the ten character traits and practices in the following chapters is that it will penetrate so deeply within us that the life, message, and mission of Jesus will be undeniable in our midst. Pragmatics will come, but let's chip away at the heart of Jesus and go from there.

Zoom-In, Zoom-Out, Capture His Image

The book follows a straightforward format as each chapter identifies a trait or practice of Christ and puts it in historical and contemporary contexts. Using camera imagery, the title and chapter sections are set up to give readers a chance to look at the words and deeds of Christ in depth, to reflect on the current urban mission scene, and to practice each character trait in their own communities. The three sections are detailed below.

Zoom-In: The first section focuses on the text of Scripture that uncovers what Christ did and taught, and gives historical, theological, and cultural background from the Gospels. It is this piece that brings the foundation for all mission practice in order to reflect Jesus in the city.

Zoom-Out: Contemporary issues from Pittsburgh, Minneapolis, Chicago, and Fresno are brought out here with an emphasis on ethnic communities. The contemporary setting establishes context for the traits and practices of Jesus that we discuss within every chapter.

Capture His Image: Here lies the application of each chapter, which is expressed through taking our contemporary context, biblical foundations, and developing action steps to capture the image of Christ. To move from theory and awareness of the problem to biblical, practical solutions is the goal at the close of each chapter. It is highly encouraged that this section be completed amongst team members, ministry leaders, and co-laborers in urban work.

A Brief Backdrop of the Urban Contexts

Mission historian Stephen Neill made this statement several years back: "If everything is mission, then nothing is mission."[2] The point was that in broadening the scope of mission, clarity on the task before us is lost. Perhaps the same could be said of urban ministry. If everything is urban, then nothing is urban. Urban intellectuals, the poor, homeless, refugees, skaters, families, majority culture dwellers, immigrants—the list could go on. It would be impossible to speak broadly to the myriad of contexts that are encompassed in the city, so I speak from a unique place. I am writing from the vantage point of the urban scene from the context of immigration. The last fifteen years of my experience have mostly been in urban America amongst newly arrived refugees. My time in Nepal, the Philippines, and the Northern Mariana Islands was heavily influenced by diaspora communities that affected almost every family in those places. The two cities of

---

2. Stephen Neill, *Creative Tension* (Edinborough: London Press, 1959), 81.

Minneapolis-St. Paul and Pittsburgh, however, fill many of the pages and the perspective from which I write.

Sprinkled throughout the book are also the contexts of Fresno and Chicago. Nancy Donat and Chris Ophus have allowed me a peek into their world and assist with contextual issues in their cities. Their neighborhoods bring the Hispanic immigrant experience to the fore and have the linguistic, transient, extended family living sort of feel that make up various ethnic neighborhoods throughout the United States. Chris and Nancy have both lived in their communities for a decade and a half, and they have listened well. Their neighbors will speak powerfully into the narrative of mission in the city. Among the four cities represented here, we can start to get a glimpse of contextual realities surrounding first- and second-generation immigrants.

There is no question that the Bhutanese-Nepali refugee narrative is the most prominent contemporary story throughout the book. It is this story that has formed much of my identity and a story that is not widely known in urban mission. The reader will hopefully come away with a deeper understanding of the journey of our friends in the city, and my hope is that there is enough crossover among the various ethnic contexts to help fill in the gaps.

The story of up rootedness through forceful displacement and poverty that is driving people from their countries is a theme that is woven into the city. Last summer we had a college student named Molly come out to Pittsburgh, and she was deeply impacted by the journey of the Bhutanese-Nepali. In the mid-1800s, the Bhutanese government invited Nepali farmers to immigrate to the southern area of the country to develop agriculture. By the early 1990s, the Bhutanese-Nepalis were driven from their homeland by the government of Bhutan claiming that their Hindu religion and Nepali language were threats to the purity of the country. For the next twenty years, they found themselves stuck in limbo in refugee camps of Nepal. Ethnically and linguistically Nepali, but no residency as refugees was the story surrounding their lives.[3] Now in the US since 2008, many are finding a new identity, not only as Nepalis living in America, but as former Hindus who have experienced Jesus' salvation. Listen to Molly's words through poem:

> Bhutan
> Strangers in Bhutan—
> But by invite, and a royal one at that.
> Come, come,
> Hoe the fields, grow the crops,
> We want you, in fact.
> We went, worthy, wanted, we
> Thrived. The sky above, the acres 'round,
> Ours—our paradise we found.
> Women aging years in a day,
> Each drop of sweat, worth a story some day.
> Powerful men, playful children,
> Ours—it was ours.
> NO, they said.
> Follow our way, the way.
> Speak only our tongue,
> That which said "Come."

3. Kenan Institute of Ethics at Duke University, "Introduction to Bhutanese Refugees in Nepal," 2013, accessed April 20, 2017, http://kenan.ethics.duke.edu/uprooted-rerouted/introductions/nepal.html.

Torn—their land, our land?

Who are we? No time—

GO, they said.

Go now or die.

Strangers out of Bhutan—

But by shun, and a royal one at that.

Nepal

Strangers in Nepal—

Miles and miles by foot, we

Went, went.

Generations passed but our blood still Nepali.

In thousands we came

Home—is this home?

The river we know,

To Jhapa, we go, go.

Foreigners come

With food, clothes, camp.

But we are home?

Camp, they say—camp is home.

"Refugee" the white man speaks.

Not we, Nepali, not refugee.

Outside the camp the brown man speaks,

He, Nepali, we, refugee.

Camp—home now,

Lowest caste, we bow

Down to our brown brother.

New years, new news—

Refugees, come.

To the land of the free, come.

Strangers out of Nepal—

But by invite, and a royal one at that.

America

Strangers in America—

Land of the free,

But we are not free

To roam the acres we once plowed,

To skip and gather—not now.

But you are free, refugee.

Come, come they said but then they ask,

Where are you from?

From Bhutan,

From Nepal,

From America,

Who are we?

Strangers in every land by decree.

Nay, He says.

That voice—shh—it is louder than the rest.

Mine, He says—

You are

From me, Mine, Forever.

We believe.

We—not refugee,

Free.

Not by the land, but by He.

Strangers, now to this world,

But by invite, and a Royal one at that.[4]

Regardless of our background or how we got to the city, we are here. Some of us have come by choice, others by default. The mission of Jesus and the call of God remain. May the attitude, character, mission, and message of Jesus so saturate our hearts as you read. May the story of those in our cities bring humility. May the life of Christ, demonstrated through his incarnation, inspire our churches and ministries to reflect him in the city. His name be hallowed. His Kingdom come, on earth as it is in heaven.

---

4. Molly Brandt, "Bhutanese-Nepali Story" (poetic project presentation for Introduction to the Arts, Colorado Christian University, Lakewood, CO, December 12, 2016).

Chapter 1
REFLECTING HIS IMAGE IN MISSION

Zoom-In

"The Spirit of the Lord is on me, because he has anointed me to proclaim good news to the poor. He has sent me to proclaim freedom for the prisoners and recovery of sight for the blind, to set the oppressed free, to proclaim the year of the Lord's favor." (Luke 4:18-19)

The life and mission of Jesus are all smashed together in this Kingdom announcement. With this reading of the scroll, Jesus establishes his identity as both Messiah and Liberator; person and function are inseparable. The holistic mission of Jesus is delayed no later than Christ's initial announcement, causing readers to quickly take notice of the purpose, nature, and expectation of his coming Kingdom. Social concern oozes from the reading of the scroll here. The blind, the oppressed, and the poor are all people who would have had little to no access to freedom.[5] Jesus comes in full authority as Messiah and announces that he has come to free the oppressed and bring liberty to those imprisoned.

---

5. Harvey Perkins, "Four Bible Studies on Development in the Asian Context," *South East Journal of Asian Theology no. 21* (1980): 79-80.

Christ models for his followers a kind of holistic ministry that differs greatly from the debates that have bounced around church circles and missiological cohorts over the years. There is seemingly no contention between Word and deed in Jesus' mission. It is simultaneously fixated 100% on compassion and 100% on spiritual transformation. Darrell Gwaltney expounds on compassion and concern for the poor of his day when he writes, "The term 'poor' refers to abjectly poor or utterly destitute. The most common term used in the Hebrew Bible for *poor* carries with it the notion of economically poor but it also suggest the idea of oppression, exploitation, and suffering."[6] The litmus test for such a claim to bring freedom to the oppressed is the action of Jesus outlined in the Gospel. Did Christ indeed do the very things he professed to accomplish? We see Jesus healing the blind (John 9:1-9), making the sick well (Luke 5:18-25), spending time with the marginalized of his day with tax collectors and sinners (Matt. 9:11), and confronting the religious and political systems (Matt. 23:13-33). To ignore an incarnation that was deeply rooted in care for the poor is impossible in surveying the biblical record.

While social and political concerns do find a striking mark in the Gospels, the notion of spiritual salvation is abundantly clear in this announcement as well. Keener notes that Christ's Messiahship is introduced as Jesus embodies the very nature of

---

6. Darrell Gwaltney, "Good News for the Poor (Luke 4:18)," *Bible Commentary for the New Baptist Covenant,* August 16, 2007, accessed November 23, 2016, http://www.ethicsdaily.com/good-news-for-the-poor-luke-4-18-bible-commentary-for-the-new-baptist-covenant-cms-9316.

what he is proclaiming.[7] Just as many in Israel were held in captivity due to their own economic or political oppression, the entire condition of the human heart was depraved, thus needing a Savior. Jesus came fulfilling, announcing, and demonstrating this through the incarnation. In his emphatic pronouncement, Jesus says, "I am anointed by the Spirit to do a very specific ministry, I am a prophet who is declaring a new era of the Kingdom, and I have come to earth and will actually bring about the release I am proclaiming."[8]

Jesus is sure of who he is as Son of God, Messiah, Lord, and King. His Kingdom frees the oppressed and flips the kingdoms of this world upside down. Though many in his hometown may be second guessing his authority or pointing to Christ's biological family as disqualifiers to his mission and purpose, Jesus is unmoved. The Trinity God revealed in Jesus came announcing, demonstrating, teaching, suffering, and resurrecting. Person and mission, both temporal and eternal, are never confused.

The Spirit of the Lord in Christ's Mission

Jesus' visit to the synagogue in Luke 4 has him citing Isaiah in the Spirit's empowerment for mission. Undoubtedly, the Spirit is the thrust behind the miracles, prophetic proclamation, and supernatural taking place in Christ's ministry. Throughout the New Testament, we see this connection between power for mission

---

7. Craig Keener, *The IVP Bible Background Commentary: New Testament* (Downers Grove, IL: InterVarsity Academic, 1993), Kindle Location 3490.

8. Darrel Bock, *Luke: The NIV Application Commentary from Biblical Text to Contemporary Life* (Grand Rapids: Zondervan, ePub 2014), 137.

and the Spirit's enablement. Notably in Luke 4, however, is the link between speaking on behalf of those who have no voice in the name of the Lord[9] and evidences of divine, inexplicable acts of Christ. Though Jesus was fully God, he emptied himself to serve and depended on the Holy Spirit to fuel the mission before him.

Luke has a unique perspective on the work of the Spirit in mission, as he is the only Gospel writer who points to the descent of the Holy Spirit as the initiation of anointing; constituting that Jesus is the Messiah, the Living Christ. Further, Luke carries out this significance of the Spirit's work in mission by outlining the Spirit as the one who empowers, inspires, and directs all Jesus said and did.[10] The implications that this has for the mission of Christ cannot be overstated as dependence on the Holy Spirit is not merely a philosophical or theoretical emptying of himself. Christ comes to earth, lays equality with God down, and has a single-minded focus as Savior, Liberator, and King. While identity or purpose of mission is never in question, this does not nullify Christ's complete dependence on the Holy Spirit to fuel his work.

One chapter earlier, the dramatic anointing at Jesus' baptism cannot be forgotten. This event was a holy moment to behold and in Jesus announcing his anointing of the Spirit, he is merely reiterating what had taken place in Luke 3. Most striking to this anointing of the Spirit is the particular kind of mission that was being envisioned. N.T. Wright comments that for Jesus'

---

9. Earl Creps, "Finding Your Prophetic Voice," (lecture, Assemblies of God Theological Seminary Chapel, Springfield, MO, April 2006).

10. Roger Stronstad, "The Holy Spirit in Luke-Acts," *Paraclete 23* no. 2 (Spring 1989): 20-22.

audience, he is simply freeing the wrong people;[11] he omits the "day of vengeance" clause from Isaiah's original prophecy in Isaiah 61 and this would not have been "Good News" to the hearers. By Jesus omitting the judgment towards the Gentiles, he includes all people, even those his listeners despised, in God's freedom and salvation. The kind of mission the Spirit is enabling is one that is counter-cultural, Spirit-infused, and brings about release instead of judgment for all.[12] The anointing and fullness of the Spirit does not merely increase personal piety or determination, but it undergirds the entire subversive mission of the Messiah.

When we model Christ's example in urban mission, it must be realized that the anointing and Spirit of the Lord in us does not guarantee acceptance from others nor grants ministry success. As soon as Jesus finishes reading the scroll, his hearers turn on him, become incredibly angry, and even try to throw him off a cliff. As we see in the life and mission of Jesus though, he lets the chips fall where they may and stays true to who he is and what he has set out to accomplish.

The Year of Jubilee

Israel had long heard of "the year of the Lord" when all debts would be forgiven and slaves would be able to start afresh with a blank slate. These words would have resounded in hearts and ears. Years of study and application have been put into these verses surrounding liberation. An entire stream of theology—

---

11. N.T. Wright, *Luke for Everyone: The New Testament for Everyone* (Louisville, KY: Westminster John Knox Press, 2004), 46-47.

12. Walt Russell, "The Anointing with the Holy Spirit in Luke-Acts," *Trinity Journal 202* (1986): 52.

liberation theology[13]—arose from this text where a strong emphasis has been placed on freedom from political or social oppression. There may be no more relevant social text for the city in our time but may we not forget that Jesus' announcement accomplishes horizontal (people to people) and vertical (people to God) liberation at the same time.[14] Jesus' deeds and actions did confront the political oppression of his day and his Kingdom addressed economic disparity, racism, slavery, and sickness amongst other issues. Christ was not mute on the issue of physical liberation, but the way he demonstrated such justice was through Calvary's love, laying down his life.[15]

Without hearts being set free through the salvation that Christ brings, we are left with a mission unfinished. Christopher Wright reminds us that the mission of Jesus was not content with liberating slaves but also reclaiming worshippers.[16] People needed a Savior and were long awaiting for a King not just to deliver them from earthly oppression but to bring them into fellowship with God. Regardless of whether the people of Christ's day could understand this deep need or not, God sent his Son to accomplish

---

13. Gustavo Gutierrez, *A Theology of Liberation*, rev. ed. (Maryknoll, NY: Orbis, 2012). This classic work on liberation theology paints the backdrop of this contextual theology as it relates to Luke 4 and the voice of the poor. Too far or not far enough is the debate, yet this book stands alone as critical for understanding liberation theology.

14. John Caufey, "To Release the Oppressed: Reclaiming a Biblical Theology of Liberation" in *Jubilee Centre,* accessed November 23, 2016, http://www.jubilee-centre.org/to-release-the-oppressed-reclaiming-a-biblical-theology-of-liberation-by-john-coffey/.

15. Gregory Boyd, *The Myth of a Christian Nation: How the Quest for Political Power is Destroying the Church* (Grand Rapids, MI: Zondervan, 2005), 29-35.

16. Christopher J.H. Wright, *The Mission of God* (Downers Grove, IL: InterVarsity Press, 2006).

this very mission. A proper self-image of who Jesus was as Messiah kept him narrowly focused on his task and ultimately glorifying his Father in heaven.

Again, the Jubilee brings to the fore the dichotomy that we have erected in recent times. Who were the poor, the blind, and the oppressed? Were these spiritual or physical slaves? Historically and theologically the arrow points in both directions. Jesus' mission and his example show that the "favor of the Lord" was for both the physically and spiritually downtrodden. For Jesus, this never has been an either/or question. He came to free the physically and spiritually oppressed, and this message and holistic mission bleeds from every page of the Gospels.

Following Jesus in Identity and Mission

Understanding that the fullness of Christ is rooted in this pronouncement in Luke 4 is pivotal to our delivery of Christ's mission. The identity and mission of Christ as Messiah are inseparable—because he is the Messiah, he does the mission. And he does the very mission he sets out to do because he is the Messiah. As we look at the life of Christ here, it is important to not encapsulate the totality of the mission of the Church and all practical theology from a few verses in Luke. That misses the point of the task before us. We are looking at the life of Christ, his words, his actions, and we are doing all we can to reflect that image to the world. Clearly, Jesus was Liberator and Messiah. He came announcing and demonstrating these both spiritually and socially. The salvation of humanity hinges on Christ's Messiahship and the very authenticity of his work as Savior is legitimized by him following through on the actions he proclaims. He does this and so much more, and this is precisely why you and I have followed him to the city to mirror his mission.

But what does it mean to have a Christ-centered identity of purpose and mission mixed together when you are not Jesus? A question that was posed by Jude Tiersma Watson in a chapter she wrote in *God So Loves the City* over twenty-two years ago has stuck with me over the years. In the fall of 2000 as a Bible college student, I read her chapter on "What does it mean to be incarnational when we are not the Messiah?"[17] It has continually challenged me to have a healthy view of what it means to engage in Christlike mission. So much of the question revolves around our own idea of being "sent" people as urban missionaries and aligning our ministry with the words and actions of Jesus. May we ponder and respond to the hard questions as we peer into our contemporary context and discuss the mission of Christ amongst friends, neighbors, and ministry partners.

Zoom-Out

Nara looked straight ahead at the TV playing an epic Nepali film when he said to me in a monotone voice, "I don't know, John. Time is not on my side. Eighteen years in a refugee camp and now I am here starting all over. No English. No job. What can I do?" He went on to tell me of the struggles of walking down the street and people shouting at him to go back to his country. Four years in and this new life in America didn't seem to be getting easier. His son and daughter-in-law seemed to be

---

17. Jude Tiersma, "What does it mean to be incarnational when we are not the Messiah?" in *God So Loves the City,* rev. ed. by Charles Van Engen and Jude Tiersma (Eugene, OR: Wipf and Stock, 2009), 14-25.

finding some sort of niche in their community. His grandkids were adjusted to school and had already become fluent in English. Nara and his wife, however, spent their days tucked away in an apartment in a rough area of St. Paul, MN, feeling pretty disconnected from the outside world.

As I talked with other Bhutanese-Nepali community leaders about Nara's situation, they lamented that this is the case for so many elders in the community.[18] They have had a loss of identity and their only real purpose is to give an opportunity to future generations. Nara and his wife had been attending ESL classes for a couple years twice a week, and still they had made little progress. The Jehovah's Witnesses and Mormons were often invited into their home just because it gave them a little dignity of feeling like they belong in America. It wasn't uncommon for Nara and folks his age to sit around and talk about the good ol' days in Bhutan before they were forced out. One day Nara's eyes lit up with joy when he began to describe the farm he and his family used to own in their small village back home. "Oranges, corn, rice, cows, goats. We had it all. It was a simple life, but it was a good life. Those years in the camp were a struggle, but now we are here. It is good. We have an apartment. Our kids have an education. Our family even has a car . . . but . . ." Nara and his wife began to cry. "That life is gone," they both moaned.

Through my tears and with a crack in my voice, I reminded Nara and his wife of the newfound faith and hope they have in

---

18. Casey Tolan, "A Mysterious Mental Health Disorder is Afflicting Bhutanese Refugees in America," *Fusion Magazine,* June 6, 2016, accessed November 23, 2016, http://fusion.net/story/310750/bhutan-refugees-pittsburgh-mental-health/. Older Bhutanese show signs of depression that are off the grid in diagnosis. Symptoms range from having pain all over their body, staring out the window appearing lost, checking out from daily chores, and disengaging from social interaction.

Christ. They are new believers and extremely committed to Jesus. Though they are in their mid-seventies now, their days are filled with house fellowships, women's prayer on Fridays, and Sunday church as well as a monthly Christian conference or two. Reflecting on what they had lost was sobering, but somehow, in God's grace, they had gained new life in Christ. Jesus had been on a mission to find them and that is what they had to cling to in these moments.

The life of forceful displacement followed by sitting idle in a refugee camp for years has taken a toll on many of my neighbors. Purpose and identity have been zapped from the lives of most community elders. The younger generation is conflicted about being American or Nepali, which language to speak when, and this quasi American-Nepali thing is not exactly their idea of a fun day.[19] But, this is the life that has unfolded for our community, and for the most part they are doing amazingly well and taking it in stride. As we look around American cities today, these stories are not uncommon. Identity crisis is here to stay, leaving many grappling to find purpose amid a culture that spins forward at an incredible rate.

Missionary Identity and Focus

Missionaries in such contexts do not find themselves excluded from these realities. We are often asked to devote years to language study, and mission necessitates that we cross cultural barriers to live in community with our urban neighbors. About

---

19. Ken Carlson, *Effective English Ministry: Reaching the Next Generation in Ethnic Immigrant Churches* (Kenneth Carlson Self-Published, 2015), Kindle Location 478-850. Drawing from doctoral research, Carlson explains the confusion linguistically and culturally for young immigrants growing up in America. Bhutanese-Nepalis are experiencing this shift at an accelerated rate

once a week I am asked by Nepali believers and Hindus what I do for a living. I have explained this many times before. I'm a pastor. I'm a volunteer that gets paid. I'm a social worker. I do community development. I'm a college professor. I'm unemployed. I research language and culture twenty-four hours a day. What line am I going to give today? Depending on my mood or optimism, my answer changes I guess. The constant questioning and inquiries to validate our lives can leave us feeling alone or as if our mission has no purpose.

I am blind. I carry a white cane, use a text to speech computer and iPhone, and read braille. My eyes look normal they say, and I'm often told I don't look blind. I'm not entirely sure what that means, but people like to say it a lot. I find my way around the city with relative ease as people are pretty helpful most of the time. Occasionally people do not know their right from left, but you can't have it all. Blindness is part of my identity that gets jumbled in with Christ-follower, missionary, urban dweller, father, and husband. When people ask me if I work in my Pittsburgh neighborhood, it isn't a simple question without ulterior motives. Are you disabled? Do you get a disability check? You mean your wife doesn't support you financially? You only do ministry work? That is it? Knowing whose you are and what you are is extremely important in my world.

When we choose to move into an urban context and be salt and light amongst our neighbors, no one really tells you ahead of time that you will be forced to come to grips with being an outsider.[20] Recently, I was sitting with a handful of urban mission

---

20. Marilyn R. Gardner, *Between Worlds: Essays on Culture and Belonging* (Doorlight Publications, 2014), Kindle Location 465-639. Gardner

leaders who all live in ethnic communities throughout the US. Most of us operate in a foreign language, and we were whining about the perpetual difficulty of being outsiders. Linguistically and culturally we have found acceptance, but there remains a learning curve, often producing feelings of inadequacy and deep loneliness. Being misunderstood by both majority and minority cultures often seems to be the norm. An understanding of who we are as "sent" people is sometimes the only thing that pushes us through the day.

Mission Identity Crisis

The waters are further muddied if the very mission that we are bringing lacks clarity. The needs of the city are too great for us to focus on them all; even within a narrow focus such as gangs, Nepalis, refugees, or the homeless, these categories are simply too broad. Without a narrow scope and plan for how ministry is carried out, we will find ourselves confused and conflicted about the best path forward. We have all witnessed the urban ministry leader who drives a van around town transporting people, moving furniture, and giving out groceries which is undoubtedly rooted in the goodness of his heart. The needs of those in the city are intense and the emotional energy needed can take an urban worker for a roller coaster ride, ending in the feeling of helplessness and exhaustion. Though these activities are noble, this "just find a need and fill it" approach overwhelms the urban leader, and it can lead him to walk away from the mission entirely.

Some time ago I was talking with my good friend, Todd, who has been serving in urban ministry for many years. His neighborhood is rough: drugs, crime, gangs, and teenage

---

emphasizes that identity in cross-cultural living is elusive, and we're often like chameleons blending into whatever context in which we find ourselves

pregnancies abound. The struggle and fight for joy is harder some days than others. They had entered into a season of ministry where he and his co-workers had found their niche. Despite all the challenges, they were planting churches, discipling new believers, seeing people rescued from the streets, and seeing families reunited. Todd was facing increasing pressure from higher ups in his mission organization to alter their plans. They wanted him to change what their ministry was doing to more closely align to the broader mission of the organization who was still searching and grasping for their identity as a movement. Finally, after many discussions, Todd told one of the men pouring the pressure on him, "So here is the deal. We are certain what we are doing is biblical. We are certain that it is working. We know we have heard the Spirit, and we are going to see this multiplied in cities around the globe. We're not confused about our identity or where we are going. This is what we are doing, and we know where we're headed."

Such confidence is rare amongst urban workers, especially confidence that is rooted in Scripture that has come as a result of praying, fasting, and waiting on the Lord. Using trial and error and hoping for the best can somewhat rule the day in this kind of work. That kind of chaos doesn't have to define our ministry. Jesus offers a different way: a Kingdom way in staying on mission as we teach and demonstrate the Word of God in our neighborhoods. He knew who he was, he announced his mission in Word and deed, and he continually brought his followers back to this centerpiece. We would do well to have a robust theology of Christlikeness when it comes to staying on mission and knowing our identity as urban Christ-followers.

Capture His Image

You are not Jesus. I am not Jesus. No one in your neighborhood or prominent urban ministry leader is the Messiah. Maybe you should say that to yourself out loud; put the book down, think about what you are saying and say it to yourself, "I am not the Messiah." If this is in fact true, that demands that we admit that the full weight of being incarnational in the same sense of Christ breaks down.[21] We are not going to save our communities nor are we called to do so. We are not going to die for all humanity. That has been done once and for all. I do think, though, that we can take the posture of Christ and get at the heart of the matter as it relates to mission.

Many urban workers I know as well as their neighbors struggle with their identity in the community. For those of us who have raised mission support and work in the city, this is a consistent difficulty to explain to others what we do, how we get paid, and on and on. Our neighbors are often coming from places of the globe where they have been uprooted and new life in the city has them reeling. May we root our own identity as urban missionaries in the fullness of the Holy Spirit in our lives and not in anything else. Discuss the following questions and answer honestly with a small group on your ministry team or close neighborhood friends.

---

21. It is imperative to admit that the model of incarnation is not perfect. *Christianity Today* discussed a series of articles on the pros and cons of such a model and Lingenfelter and Mayer's *Ministering Cross-Culturally* was brought into the discussion as it relates to incarnational ministry. My point is that we focus more on reflecting the example of Jesus pulling out Godward practices while not neglecting

How dependent are you on the Holy Spirit day to day? Do you believe you are getting your identity and purpose solely from him? Describe.

When you are not full of the Spirit on a day to day basis, where do you turn to find your identity and purpose? How does that play out in your life?

What do you want your neighbors in the city to know you for? Do you think this is the same identity they see in you right now?

What action steps do you need to take to go from being conflicted about your identity in the city to confidence that the Spirit has sent, enabled, and given an identity to you?

As we zoomed-in on Christ's incarnational mission, we saw that mission and identity were intricately connected. We also concluded that Christ's mission was holistic integrating spiritual salvation and social concern. If we desire to reflect Christ's image in the same way, we would do well to ensure that our ministries strike the same veins that Jesus hit in his pronouncement.

Trotter

Continue the discussion on capturing Christ's image around the theme of holistic mission.

Who are the invisible and oppressed in your community? Who does the general population consistently ignore? Whose voice is not being heard?

How are you and your ministry bringing freedom to those in your community? Give examples of how you are giving them the eternal hope of salvation as well as freedom from the plight that they may be experiencing in the here and now.

Is your church, ministry team, or mission organization on the same page when it comes to holistic mission in Christ's name? How have you or can you facilitate that conversation and call to action?

What challenges are you facing personally and on your ministry team as you attempt to stay faithful to this mission?

What practical steps can you take to instill this mission identity into your neighbors—moving them from city dwellers just getting by from day to day to sent people, full of the Spirit, engaged in mission?

How accessible are you to the marginalized in your community? How does your lifestyle or living situation make it possible for community members to know you deeply?

Jesus left the comforts of heaven and made his dwelling among us here on earth. He modeled holistic mission for us showing that his identity as Messiah and clarity of mission were certain. We too have moved into urban neighborhoods, or perhaps God will call you to live in the city. It is imperative that we have confidence in our identity as sent people and that our mission is rooted in Scripture. We are not Jesus. We are not the Messiah, and we will never be able to fully incarnate who he is nor should we. But, we do have a beautiful example that pushes us to evaluate our spiritual lives and mission statements and to refocus us on the centerpiece of the gospel.

We can make all the right decisions about practical concerns of identifying with our neighbors, but we may still completely miss the mark on capturing his image in mission. Perhaps we send our child to neighborhood schools, take years to learn Nepali, Spanish, or Chinese to better communicate with neighbors, buy a home in the prime location of our neighborhood—still, if we fail to be full of the Spirit and have a mission that is rooted in Jesus' words and deeds, we will not capture the image of Christ.

May the realigning of our identity and mission propel us in the days ahead as we seek to reflect his image in preaching the Good News to the poor, giving sight to the blind, and setting the captives free.

Chapter 2
REFLECTING HIS IMAGE IN PRAYER AND REST

Zoom-In

Very early in the morning, while it was still dark, Jesus got up, left the house and went off to a solitary place, where he prayed. Simon and his companions went to look for him, and when they found him, they exclaimed: "Everyone is looking for you!" Jesus replied, "Let us go somewhere else—to the nearby villages—so I can preach there also. That is why I have come." (Mark 1:35-38)

The apostles gathered around Jesus and reported to him all they had done and taught. Then, because so many people were coming and going that they did not even have a chance to eat, he said to them, "Come with me by yourselves to a quiet place and get some rest." So they went away by themselves in a boat to a solitary place. (Mark 6:30-32)

The paradox found in the incarnation of Jesus regarding prayer is that Jesus seemed to continually be taking time for those in great need while concurrently getting away to a solitary place to pray. This tension was undoubtedly felt and the pull in both directions is abundant in the Gospels. There are more than twenty-five accounts of Jesus withdrawing to a place of solitude with Mark delineating nine such occurrences alone. Jesus prays while it is still dark (Mark 1:35). He often withdrew to lonely places to pray as crowds followed him (Mark 1:45; Mark 4:1; Luke 5:15-16). He went alone and also took his disciples with him to quiet places to pray (Mark 2:13; Mark 3:7; Matt. 14:13; Luke 9:18). He went to a mountainside to get away and once prayed alone all night (Luke 6:12-13; Mark 3:13; Mark 6:46; Matt. 15:29; Mark 9:2; Luke 22:39). Jesus often walks alone and spends time in solitude (John 7:10; John 10:39-41; Luke 9:51). Jesus tries to get his disciples to pray with him at Gethsemane (Mark 14:32). Alone, with the disciples, sitting, walking, preaching sermons, discussing hard truths—Jesus reflected prayer with his entire being.

Solitude Has Never Been Easy

Urban life and all its glitter can often feel like a completely different world compared to Jewish society of the first century. The setting in which Jesus finds himself, however, has many of the same pressures of our time. Ancient Israel would have had four homes facing a shared courtyard and as many as twenty people could have been living in the common area of each residence.[22] This was further complicated by villages being connected to each other with crowded streets and people rising before the sun rose to start their work. The communal nature of such villages demanded constant interaction and interruption. Jesus' example in Mark 1 reminds us that there is a costly sacrifice in time alone with the Father. For Christ, perhaps this was the only time of the day for him to receive solitude with the one who had sent him.

---

22. Keener, Kindle Location 2312.

Conn and Ortiz argue that Jesus' ministerial attention on surrounding villages and towns can miscommunicate that Christ had a much greater focus on rural areas. That is what a reading of town or village would render in contemporary English. The reality is that rapid urbanization had taken place in Israel during the first century, and where Jesus ministered was one of the most densely populated areas in the Roman Empire.[23] With such assumptions on rural living, we can read the text as if Jesus walked three minutes down the trail, found a tree, and spent some time with God in solitude. Quite the contrary, the Messiah may have needed to bypass several villages and markets in the wee hours of the morning to ensure that he could get away and be with the Father. The situation of Jesus' call to come away and abide is more similar to urban contexts than we may initially presume.

In such an environment where Jesus' local village had constant demand for his attention, it is no coincidence why we see such frequency in Jesus withdrawing to pray and challenging his followers to do the same. Given that Jesus and his disciples may have needed to walk a few miles out to find a "lonely" place makes the frequency and call of the Scripture that much more applicable to our day. The city is calling, ministry never stops we say, but Christ got away to a lonely place to be with his Father.

The Pendulum Between Prayer and Mission

In Mark 1:35-39, Jesus is found alone praying by his disciples, and his response to their demands for ministry is one of compassion and patience. Jesus responds by reaffirming his

---

23. Harvie M. Conn and Manuel Ortiz, *Urban Ministry: The Kingdom, the City, and the People of God* (Downers Grove, IL: IVP, 2001), 119-121.

commission to preach the gospel to the surrounding towns and villages. Henri Nouwen illuminates this sort of swinging of the pendulum from solitude, to community, and to ministry when he writes of the rhythm of abiding with the Father and pouring out again in ministry.[24] While there is no question that Jesus had a very specific purpose in mind as he modeled getting alone to pray, he does not make prayer life into something so rigid that it forsakes mission.[25] Drawing back to his overall purpose in coming to earth, prayer is certainly the fuel that avails him to the Spirit's work while mission flows out of such time in the wilderness.

The disciples come to Jesus in chapter 1 of Mark asserting the need to get back on mission. Jesus does not respond that he is busy praying or cannot be bothered. He immediately connects their request back to the original mission we discussed from Luke 4. He has been sent to preach to the neighboring towns and villages which is why he promptly ends his prayer and lets the pendulum swing back to community and ministry. There does not seem to be a great deal of tension for the Messiah to switch gears from abiding with the Father, socializing with disciples, and healing the sick and demon-possessed in the crowd.[26] Perhaps a

---

24. Henri Nouwen, "Solitude, Community, Ministry," in *Leadership Journal*, Spring 1995.

25. Though Jesus only had three years to accomplish his mission, he continually models getting alone in solitude to pray. Concluding that Jesus neglected prayer for mission is not what I wish to communicate. Rather, the pendulum swings back and forth and the example Jesus set was maneuvering in and out of these modes with great patience.

26. Jenny Williams, "Jenny Williams: Our Interruptions Are Our Work," in *Faith and Leadership,* August 4, 2009, accessed December 15, 2016, https://www.faithandleadership.com/jenny-williams-our-interruptions-are-our-work. Reiterating Nouwen's admonition to flow with interruptions, Williams

foundational point for us in living in Christlikeness in the city is to become more and more comfortable with interruptions, random socializing, and ministry demands. This is all precipitated, however, by extravagant time in solitude with God. The pendulum goes back and forth, back and forth, and back and forth . . . and Jesus stays on mission with God the entire time.

Mark 6 further clarifies this pendulum swinging between solitude, community, and ministry when the disciples try to escape to a lonely place but are interrupted by huge crowds. Robert Stein comments on the situation in writing of the crowds' ability to follow Jesus and the disciples to their place of rest—yes, even in the desert the Messiah was found.[27] Though rest would have been ideal, Jesus responds to the crowds because he realizes they are sheep without a shepherd. Yet again, the disciples forsake what they know to be true. They are in the presence of God incarnate, in the presence of the Messiah. They shift their focus from this and try to feed 5,000 people by natural means.

In Jesus' teaching on prayer and ministry, however, he shows the disciples that the Kingdom of God has come. The poor who never are well fed find their fill through the supernatural multiplication of food, and the disciples learn the spiritual lesson that prayer precedes the miraculous.[28] The adrenaline of the crowd was undoubtedly intoxicating. Witnessing thousands of people living in poverty find sustenance is a miracle unlike any of us has ever seen. Still, the call is to the wilderness. Immediately

---

builds the case that the entire ministry of Christ was one interruption after another. Likewise is the work of the ministry.

27. Robert Stein, *Mark: Baker Exegetical Commentary on the New Testament* (Grand Rapids, MI: Baker Academic, 2008), Kindle Location 8114.

28. Ibid., 8279-80.

before this amazing event and many times after, Jesus is called and continually calls his disciples to go away to a solitary place to rest and pray.

A Corporate Call to Get Away

The American cultural packaging of the gospel often assumes individualizing the teachings and patterns of Jesus: personal salvation, personal repentance, individual fasting, and most certainly personal prayer.[29] While these can have their place in being crafted into better disciples, may we not move too quickly away from reflecting Jesus in the city in regard to corporate time away with the Father. Mark 6 is one of many examples wherein Christ calls his disciples to come away with him and rest. They do not go alone; they come as a band of disciples, as a ministry team to a place of isolation and solitude.

The Lord's Prayer and the disciples asking Jesus to teach them to pray have drawn much attention in both devotional and scholarly writing.[30] But what can be said of reflecting Jesus in the way he invited his followers to pray with him? Certainly, the disciples heard the actual words that Jesus spoke when he prayed, listened to the silence as Christ waited on the Spirit, or saw with

---

29. Scott McKnight, N.T. Wright, and Dallas Willard, *The King Jesus Gospel: The Original Good News Revisited,* rev. ed. 2016. (Grand Rapids, MI: Zondervan), 29-30. McKnight distinguishes between the overall message of the Kingdom (discussed in part in chapter 2 of this book) and personal salvific benefits that we receive. John Piper, N.T. Wright, and blogger/pastor Andy Fuqua all make similar comments on the individualization of the gospel to the detriment of Christian community and Kingdom living.

30. Much attention is given to the disciples asking Jesus to teach them to pray while they never asked for instruction in preaching, teaching, or serving in other areas of ministry. Further, the Catholic tradition on the Lord 's Prayer and scholarly works focuses on the content of what Jesus prayed. The emphasis here, however, is the corporate pattern and imitation that precedes teaching.

their own eyes the exhaustion that came over their Rabbi as he prayed until blood arose from his perspiration (Luke 22:44). There is no greater classroom than walking with the Teacher himself.

The life of Christ modeled time and again bringing his followers to solitary places to pray together. When Jesus brought his followers with him to the place of rest and when the disciples asked Jesus to teach them to pray, they invited themselves into the prayer life of Jesus. As always, N.T. Wright says it better than most:

Its [the Lord's Prayer] shape and content remind us of the public career of Jesus at every point. And since Jesus' public career was solidly rooted and reflected in his own life of prayer, we must conclude that the Lord's Prayer is an invitation to share Jesus' own prayer life—and with it his agenda, his work, his pattern of life, and his spirituality. The Lord's Prayer marks out Jesus' followers as a distinct group not simply because Jesus gave it to them, but because it encapsulates his own mission and vocation. And it does this in a form appropriate for his followers, which turns them into his co-workers and fellow laborers in prayer for the Kingdom.[31]

Zoom-Out

Sirens blaring, music thumping, children chattering in foreign languages, the outlining of downtown lights in the background—urban life puts the senses on overload. The city

---

31. N.T. Wright, "The Lord's Prayer as a Paradigm of Christian Prayer" in *Into God's Presence: Prayer in the New Testament*, ed. R.L. Longenecker (Grand Rapids, MI: Eerdmans, 2001), 132-54.

brings people from all over the world to its borders because of the great opportunity it provides in so many areas of life. Access to education, development, and career often begin on its doorstep.[32] Such an environment calls for busyness and noise that many have never known. In fact, being busy has become a cultural phenomenon that some newcomers to the US try to emulate.

I recall Bhutanese refugees coming to Minneapolis-St. Paul in 2008 during the heart of the US economic recession. Jobs were not available, children had not started the new school year yet, and onlookers could find groups of Bhutanese sitting on the grass outside apartment complexes resembling the refugee camp life they had experienced for the previous two decades.[33]

Within a couple months, the typical greeting went from "How are you? I'm fine," to "How are you? I'm so busy." In reality, no one was very busy. There was simply nothing to do, but they had quickly learned that American culture establishes busyness as a sign of progress and development.

In late March of 2016, I was experiencing my first spring in Pittsburgh. The snow had melted away, and kids were about a foot taller when they emerged from their homes after a winter of being trapped inside. My Nepali neighbor was sitting on his porch, and he called me over to sing along to the guitar with him late at night. All our neighbors had gone inside for the evening when Hari began

---

32. Ray Bakke, *A Theology As Big As The City* (Downers Grove, IL: IVP, 1997), Kindle Location 65-70. Bakke lays out the push and pull factors of urbanization delineating the "magnet" contained in the urban context.

33. Bhutanese refugees began arriving in the US from refugee camps in Nepal in 2008. The previous eighteen years were spent in camps with no employment and life was characterized by sitting around, colloquially called "refugee life."

to comment on the busyness of life in America. "No one really stops by to see us anymore. When something was happening, good or bad, in my country, everything stopped.[34] Now it is just very lonely. There is just no time because of all the pressure." I sat in silence reflecting on the transition I had seen over the last eight years in the Nepali community in urban America. Hari was right, and the admonition I heard years ago rang true: beware of the barrenness of a busy life.

Prayer in Chicago

Ministry demands a lot of focus from the urban leader, and there is a constant call for our attention. In the introduction, I briefly mentioned the neighborhood of Little Village in Chicago explaining that my friend Chris and his entourage would help us understand the Hispanic context throughout the book. Chris's pastor, Paco, has taught Chris and his family over the years the deep value of getting alone with the Father. It is not uncommon for the ministry to enter into weeklong fasts wherein all are encouraged to call on the name of the Lord. During a phone conversation, Chris commented to me that this has been one of the most significant marks on him and his family in fifteen years of ministry.

To someone looking in from the outside, they may remark that Little Village is just another blighted, gang infested, rough neighborhood. For Chris's church and many partner organizations, however, time alone with the Father has shown them otherwise.

---

34. Funerals and weddings in the Nepali community call for a one to two week freezing of all other activities. The death of this rhythm of life was being lamented.

Teenage Girls in Crisis as Prayer Partners in Fresno

Nancy Donat has lived in Fresno for seventeen years now. Single and full of the Spirit, Nancy bought a large house not long after relocating, and her place has become a haven for many teenage girls who find themselves in difficult circumstances. Nancy recalls that some of the most powerful moments over all these years have been times when she is at her wit's end, and teenagers living at her place asked if they could pray with her. Chatting with her by phone this winter, she retold a story of when a girl simply asked if she could pray for Nancy. The teacher-student relationship was turned upside down as one of the most unlikely people became a vessel of transformation through prayer. Over and over, Nancy says, "These moments have happened and become defining moments in my own discipleship."

Bhutanese-Nepali Crying Out to God

My neighbor Santosh is twenty-one years old, and we have become like surrogate parents to him as he is pretty much on his own. He came to the States when he was fifteen with few family connections. He tells of the experience of refugee camps in Nepal experiencing a massive outpouring of God's Spirit and hundreds of Hindu folks coming to the Lord.[35] It was often young people who

---

35. Danielle Priess, "Why Nepal Has One Of The World's Fastest-Growing Christian Populations," *NPR, Stories of Life in a Changing World*, February 3, 2016, accessed December 21, 2016, http://www.npr.org/sections/goatsandsoda/2016/02/03/463965924/why-nepal-has-one-of-the-worlds-fastest-growing-christian-populations. In 1951, Nepal had zero recorded Christians. By 1961, the number of Christians recorded was 458. By 2011, the number of Christians recorded was 375,000. The country's population is under 30 million. Many believe these numbers are actually much higher but inaccurately reported.

experienced this wave of the gospel. Santosh said, "When I came to the Lord, me and my friends used to spend all night praying together. We would go with our pastor and stay inside the church and just spend all night praising, worshipping, and praying to God. I can never forget that time."[36]

This type of electric atmosphere is commonplace when you sit and talk with Nepali believers here in Pittsburgh. Many have come to Christ only recently, and a major part of their decision to leave the Hinduism they had known was because people prayed for God to show himself strong through miraculous signs.[37] God answered. Now, their worlds have been flipped upside down in a very different way as they cope with the busyness of life in the United States. The demands of the city are competing for the attention of many Bhutanese-Nepali believers these days. Santosh's story of getting alone to the secret place to pray and miraculous signs birthed in prayer will become stories of yesteryear if the kindling is not reignited in American cities.

Silence in the City

We all stand behind a long line of people who have given their lives to Jesus and followed him to the city. People have

---

36. Meg Batarai, interview by author via telephone, February 12, 2016.

37. Joe Mohan, "Church in Nepal is Growing Rapidly," *Calvin Chimes,* March 12, 2014, accessed December 1, 2016, http://www.calvin.edu/chimes/2014/03/12/church-in-nepal-is-growing-rapidly/. Rev. Manoj Shrestha, Princeton PhD candidate (at the time of this article and former Bible college president in Nepal), attributes the amazing growth of the Nepali church to the work of the Holy Spirit. He says the church in Nepal resembles the first century where there is persecution alongside great excitement for God, healings, and exorcisms. This matches the pulse and experience of Bhutanese-Nepali Christians in the US

wrestled for the place of solitude as they are surrounded by the hustle and bustle of their neighborhood. Jude Tiersma Watson has spent over two decades in LA, and she describes rest well: "I used to think that Sabbath rest was for the purpose of working harder and being able to keep up the next week. But God did not rest so that he could create more. He ceased, stopped, and told us to do the same. When I do this, I am reminded that ministry does not belong to us but to God."[38] Though in the moment it may appear that excessive going will keep everything moving along, it is just a matter of time before the wheels come off and the entire mission is aborted. God rested. He ceased.

Nancy, after nearly thirty years now in urban ministry, has talked about regularly getting away to places of solitude. When I look at the longevity she has had in urban work, it is no coincidence that getting away has been a sustaining discipline for her. Unplugging is an ongoing challenge in our contemporary settings, and stillness remains a bit out of our grasp. Every time I call Nancy to check in with her, some level of chaos has just taken place on her block or in the life of someone close to her. She reflects the admonition of Mother Teresa so well. "In the silence of the heart, God speaks. If you face God in prayer and silence, God will speak to you. Then you will know that you are nothing. It is only when you realize your nothingness, your emptiness, that God can fill you with himself. Souls of prayer are souls of great silence."[39]

---

38. Jude Tiersma Watson, "Journey from Obedience to Joy" in *Global Missiology* (October 2012).

39. Mother Teresa, *In the Heart of the World,* accessed December 3, 2016, http://www.newworldlibrary.com/NewWorldLibraryUnshelved/tabid/767/articleType/ArticleView/articleId/19/Mother-Teresa-on-Silence.aspx.

Capture His Image

The call of your neighborhood will never go away. There is always one more conversation to be had, one more practical need to fill. The invitation to come and abide with Jesus is available to us anytime day or night. As we see in the life of Jesus, we will be interrupted. Those interruptions can turn into some of the most amazing opportunities to display God's Kingdom, and great sensitivity to the Spirit must be in place. Knowing how to bounce back and forth between the pendulum of solitude, community, and ministry is a dance that few have mastered. This, however, is the transformative work that Christ has set before us. He has modeled this life to the finest degree and has invited us to do the same.

About once every three months or so, my wife Charity and I have to come back to this abiding, rest, and ministry conversation. After fifteen years of ministry, we still struggle greatly in knowing when to get away, when to hang out with people, and when to put the pedal to the metal and go with ministry endeavors. The door to our home is always open and several days a week we can have people here until late in the evening. We have made these choices. We have agreed as a family to such a life of ministry. Having this conversation in the context of your family or ministry team is critical. We are certainly called to get away for rest and prayer, but this will affect the lives of many in your neighborhood. May we ask honest questions with Spirit-inspired solutions together. Let us look first at the personal prayer call in reflecting Jesus in our city.

Trotter

Do you have a time and place that you get away on a daily basis to rest and pray? Describe that place and what you do during these times.

In recent days, what has the Holy Spirit been showing you and teaching you in your place of solitude? What have you done or what are you doing in response to his voice?

What distractions do you need to clear in order to give God your full attention during times of prayer or fasting?

Oftentimes rest is seen as weakness not strength. How will you ensure that those you are leading know that it is necessary and beneficial to rest? What restructuring is required in your current ministry to make rest a priority for all on your team?

The life and example of Jesus calls for solitude, community, and ministry to coexist. American culture is pretty good at compartmentalizing sections of our lives to ensure that activities or functions do not blur together. The model before us, however, doesn't make such clear distinctions and the call to rest and pray often means that we will be interrupted by socializing or ministry demands. There is no black and white answer to this dance, but it is critical that your family and ministry team understand one another's threshold with this pendulum. Again, none of this ever works perfectly. Urban life and ministry is not a science. Talk honestly together and discuss moving between solitude, community, and ministry.

What day of the week have you set aside personally or as a family for solitude? Do your neighbors or friends understand that this is your day of rest?

Describe your personality and threshold for social interaction. Do you enjoy being around people often? Describe the other members on your team. How do you see them functioning in terms of socializing and ministry demands?

How do you deal with interruptions? How do you generally respond when you are interrupted when you are praying? How do you respond when you are interrupted when socializing or doing programmed ministry?

What are some action steps you can take to improve your ability to go back and forth from solitude, to community, to ministry with the compassion and patience of Christ?

If you could tell your teammates three things to help you better thrive in these areas, what would you tell them?

Pray together and ask God to help each of you in these areas of the dance of solitude, community, and ministry.

Discipleship expressed in prayer and rest does not happen in complete isolation. While we are called to personally get away to be with the Father, we are also called to model prayer among those we are discipling. Let these last few discussion points serve as an evaluation on how you are doing in terms of bringing people together to pray and of modeling a life of prayer and rest.

How often do you bring those on your ministry team together to pray? How are you being challenged to improve this practice?

Have you ever experienced someone older in the faith showing you how to pray? Describe the experience and what you gained from it.

Write down a list of two to four people who you are directly influencing that you can invite to pray with you on a regular basis. Describe to the group your plan of action and ask them to hold you accountable.

To pray is to act. As we move from solitude, to community, to ministry, and back and forth between all three, we are continually being transformed to Christ's image. Reflecting Jesus in the city is not for the faint of heart, and sometimes we have to work hard in order to rest. It is a paradox that Jesus understood and modeled so well. As soon as you put this book down, or maybe even before, someone is going to text you. A knock is going to come to your door. The notification will buzz in for your next meeting. Seemingly the city never sleeps. Truly we must be aware of the barrenness of a busy life and answer the call to the place of solitude. For Jesus the road to the cross was a road marked with continual rest stops of prayer. The wooing of the Spirit has not changed, and we have a beautiful invitation before us to come to the Fountain.

Chapter 3
REFLECTING HIS IMAGE IN SUFFERING AND SACRIFICE

Zoom-In

Foundational Scriptures: Matt. 27:1-50; Luke 23:1-46

The results of sin and death rear their head from cover to cover throughout the Scriptures, and Christ demonstrates in great power what it is to overcome. In reading the story of God, it does not take very long to realize that we live in a war zone influenced by real demonic principalities and powers (Eph. 6).[40] Jesus, though he was God, was not exempt from pain and suffering. Using Luke 23 and Matthew 27, the crucifixion, as our foundational narrative for reflecting Jesus in suffering, clear the lens and refocus on these dark days of Jesus in order to greater reflect his glory in the city.

Rejection and Danger in Being Handed Over to the Authorities (Matt. 27:1-2; Luke 23:1-12)

The rejection and fear that accompanies suffering are perhaps the most pronounced emotions in the whole experience. The unknown, particularly as it relates to our own demise, leaves

---

40. Gregory Boyd, *God at War: The Bible and Spiritual Conflict,* Kindle ed. (Downers Grove, IL: IVP, 2014). Boyd's 400-page treatise on spiritual conflict in the Scriptures contributes greatly to this often neglected subject (especially in American Evangelicalism).

us short of breath. C.S. Lewis describes the situation well when he writes, "No one ever told me that grief felt so much like fear. I am not afraid, but the sensation is like being afraid . . . There is some sort of invisible blanket between the world and me. I find it hard to take in what anyone says."[41] When Christ is brought to the governing authorities with no real accusations, certainly the weight of rejection was more real at that point than any other time in his life.

The trial taking place as narrated in Luke's Gospel outlines three separate trials after originally meeting with the Sanhedrin. Particular governing rules are being observed because of the timing of the trials since execution is involved, thus leading to both private and public hearings.[42] Though Pilate's examination declares Jesus innocent, the proceedings continue.[43] Several accusations were thrown at Christ in these hours ranging from subverting the nation, to opposing taxes to Caesar, to claiming to be Christ the King (Luke 23:2). In the end it is the "Christ the King" charge that the authorities deliver (Luke 23:3), and when Jesus is asked if he is the Messiah he responds by saying, "You have said so."[44]

These moments are lonely hours for the Messiah. Christ is often silent, and he is even dressed in a robe to be mocked as king as he is passed back and forth between trials (Luke 23:9-11). Most notable to the suffering of Christ in this text is the rejection and

---

41. C.S. Lewis, *A Grief Observed: Collective Letters of C.S. Lewis,* Kindle ed. (1961; reprint, HarperCollins 1996), Kindle Location 178.
42. Bock, 583.

43. Ibid.

44. Ibid.

ridicule he faces. Only moments prior Peter denies that he ever knew Jesus (Luke 22:57-61) and within hours another friend will betray him for a bag of silver (Matt. 27:2-4). Intimate friends were denying Jesus at the very same time he was being taunted and mocked by the crowds; rejection was happening at every turn. The experience in urban ministry should never be assumed to have a completely different experience than our Savior. We will face ridicule. We will be rejected. We will be falsely accused. The degree to which we reflect Jesus in suffering and sacrifice may determine the measure of the authenticity of the gospel we teach.

Betrayal in the Suffering of Jesus (Matt. 27:3-10)

Betrayal is an abandonment or violation of trust of someone close to you.[45] In studying the road to the cross, it is easy to skip over the weight of betrayal Jesus must have felt. He had to be betrayed to eventually die and be resurrected to give new life to all humanity. Judas had to betray Jesus. This, however, does not undermine the loss and suffering of Jesus. Randle writes,

> [Compared to our betrayals in marriage, work, etc.] In a much more intense way, Jesus was betrayed by Judas Iscariot into the hands of the Jewish religious leaders. The mental anguish caused by the betrayal, one of Jesus' disciples and closest friends, is an often overlooked aspect of Jesus' suffering. He had invested in Judas. He

---

45. Drew Randle, "How Should We Respond to Betrayal," *Christianity Today: Christian Bible Studies*, 2013, accessed December 29, 2016, http://www.christianitytoday.com/biblestudies/bible-answers/spirituallife/how-should-we-respond-to-betrayal.html.

loved Judas. He cared intensely for Judas. He was discouraged. He hurt. He felt pain. He wept. Just like we respond in moments of betrayal.[46]

The manner in which Judas betrays Jesus hardly seems fitting of the Messiah. Trading Jesus for thirty pieces of silver was the price of selling a slave according to Old Testament records, implying that Judas sold his Master very cheaply.[47] Capture the setting in your mind. The gathering around the Lord's table would have been the most momentous of occasions, eating the food that reminded previous generations of being rescued from bondage. The meal was intimate, hence the beautiful artistic depictions of this event over the centuries. To not be present, further to betray the host during this meal, would have been scandalous.[48] Judas betrays Jesus in the cheapest, most shameful way possible. The response of Christ though, is calm, collective, and gracious. "Do what you must" is the tone we receive in the Gospels.

In the verses following, Judas hangs himself which would undoubtedly bring on further emotion in the suffering of Christ. The betrayal and now the death of a friend transpire in a matter of hours. "Do what you must do quickly" from John 13 implies that Jesus knew that he was being betrayed. It appears that Jesus has the foresight to know that the cross is swiftly coming. That obviously makes the betrayal and suffering even more difficult. To lose a friend to deception and then to physical death builds great

---

46. Ibid.

47. Keener, Kindle Location 1740.

48. Keener, Kindle Location 1733.

relational, emotional loss moments before Christ will suffer a gruesome execution.

Suffering in Physical Pain of Flogging and Mockery (Matt. 27:27-45)

Jesus was brutally tortured on a cross. The irony in this fully God, fully man Savior being nailed to a tree has baffled the minds of observers for hundreds of years. With the risk of rehashing what many have said before, I do want to look briefly at the tragic loss Jesus experienced in his beatings and death. It is imperative for us to take a closer look at the physical pain and public embarrassment Christ experienced in suffering if we wish to accurately reflect his image in pain and sacrifice. The goal, of course, is not fascination or marveling at torture but we want to identify with Christ in his suffering (Phil. 3) in order that greater worship arises in us.

Most criminals were crucified on t-shaped style crosses and tradition holds that this was true for the Messiah.[49] Generally, the criminal's cross was planted in the ground just outside the city. These areas would have been high-trafficked areas and were intended to deter passersby from doing crime.[50] After prisoners were sentenced to be crucified, they were stripped down and forced to walk naked through the streets carrying their crosses which typically weighed between 100-200 pounds. Flogging and scourging were required to happen prior to crucifixion according

---

49. Mark A. Marinella, *Died He For Me: A Physician's View of the Crucifixion of Jesus Christ* (2008; reprint, Nordskog Publishing Inc., 2016), Kindle Location 606.

50. Marinella, Kindle Location 607

to Roman law. The sight was so grotesque and the shame so humiliating that Cicero commented that the word "cross" should be removed from people's eyes, their ears, even their thoughts.[51] So obscene was crucifixion that such a topic would never be discussed in any kind of social gathering.

The public shame that took place for Jesus can hardly be overstated. In the latter moments of crucifixion, the bowels of the one on the cross would open up, creating a despicable sight in addition to the already battered body among the crowds.[52] There are a couple opinions on the wine that Jesus received by force as he was dying. Some have commented that it provided temporary relief while others assert that it was mixed with morphine to provide extended strength in order that the criminal would suffer even longer. Bock comments on the nature of such a drink as a poor man's wine, creating one more depiction of a despised, dejected, and impoverished king on the cross.[53]

Any person who was to be crucified was not only a criminal, but considered to be cursed of God (Gal. 3:13). A Jewish audience could not conceive of an Anointed One or how glory could be displayed in such an antithetical event. Beyond the public disdain and social ostracism of crucifixion, Jesus was beaten mercilessly. In scourging, a whip was generally used with small metal balls or pieces of sheep bones attached to its end. Those

---

51. Guy Davies, "Cicero on the Offense of the Cross," *Exiled Preacher, Displaced Fragments: Theology, Ministry, Interviews, and Reviews,* March 12, 2012, accessed December 30, 2016, http://exiledpreacher.blogspot.com/2012/03/cicero-on-offence-of-cross.html.

52. Johan Persyn, "The Embarrassment of Crucifixion," February 22, 2017, accessed February 23, 2017, http://www.johanpersyn.com/embarrassment-crucifixion/.

53. Bock, 595.

sharp objects would rip the skin basically shearing a person as if they were an animal. Here is an analysis of the abuse given by Mayo Clinic records:

When the soldiers tore the robe from Jesus' back, they probably reopened the scourging wounds. The severe scourging, with its intense pain and appreciable blood loss, most probably left Jesus in a pre-shock state. Moreover, hematidrosis had rendered his skin particularly tender. The physical and mental abuse meted out by the Jews and the Romans, as well as the lack of food, water, and sleep, also contributed to his generally weakened state.[54]

Lastly, Jesus was beaten so badly he could hardly be recognized (Isa. 50:6; 52:14). He was blindfolded, beaten, and would not be able to roll with the punches (Mark 14:65). After beating him with a rod on the head, Roman soldiers placed a crown of thorns on this tender area of his body. Following the scourging noted above, Jesus was beaten yet again (Matt. 27:26-30). Vulnerable and maligned in every sense, Christ was hanged on the cross and breathed his last.

These are the most sobering, dark pages of Scripture. Christ-followers across the miles still take the Friday of Holy Week to mourn and remember the suffering of Christ. In our embarrassment, shame, infirmity, and rejection, Christ has walked the road before us. There is absolute resurrection in his name, but there is also deep loss and suffering. As we live out the gospel in our urban contexts, we carry with us the life of Jesus that was preceded by pain and death.

---

54. "The Physical Death of Jesus Christ: Study of the Mayo Clinic," *Journal of the American Medical Association* 1986, accessed December 29, 2016, http://www.frugalsites.net/jesus/crucifixion.htm.

Don't Look Away From the Pain Too Quickly

The theology of suffering is an extensive subject that beckons reflection and much apologetic probing. C.S. Lewis, Soong-Chan Rah, Tim Keller, Walter Brueggemann, and even Soren Kierkegaard have made tremendous contributions on the subject.[55] Theologically and philosophically, these writers have helped clarify the problem of evil and suffering in our world. Innumerous biographies have been written about servants of Christ who have been willing to follow Christ in his suffering as they face tragedy, persecution, and loss. While we can continually learn from such perspectives, it is the zooming-in on the suffering of Jesus that demands our attention. Christ walked through emotional, mental, relational, spiritual, and physical suffering in his time on earth. He responded with assuredness and authority. He has set an example in every way as we attempt to follow his lead in the city.

Before rushing into practical application of these events, may we spend time zooming-in on the text of Scripture. Matthew 26-27 and Luke 22-23 deserve careful attention and reflection. Read those chapters a few times over. Take in every word, every comma, and every conversation exchange. Look and listen for the voice of Jesus in his suffering. Reflect on the themes represented in this section and catch the heart and life of Jesus afresh. It is that life and that Spirit which enable each of us to reflect his image in our neighborhoods.

---

55. Soren Kierkegaard, C.S. Lewis, and more recently Walter Brueggemann, Soong-Chan Rah, N.T. Wright, and Tim Keller have made tremendous contributions to the theology of suffering and pain. Any student wanting to grasp this subject more comprehensively would be encouraged to dive into these works. The biblical record, however, is of utmost concern in our study.

Zoom-Out

Uprootedness, loss, and suffering are scars that weave their way through the city. Stories of physical impairment, abuse, war, and abandonment accompany so many residing in urban centers. To disconnect the sacrifice and suffering of Christ from our lived experience as well as the journey of our neighbors would be a step in the wrong direction. Christ has identified with our losses on every level, and the sacrifices we endure and sometimes are called to endure take on fresh meaning when seen through the lens of the cross. Peek into the city a bit as we hear the stories of urban workers and neighbors fight for joy.[56]

Slowly Going Blind While Trying to Teach Others to See Jesus

When I was nine years old, I was told that I had a degenerative eye condition that would eventually lead to blindness. The disease, Retinitis Pigmentosa (RP), strikes in adolescence and resurfaces in waves every few years.[57] In the late nineties, I was sitting in my college library having already surrendered my driver's license due to the deterioration of my vision. I glanced up at the lights in the basement of my study area, and I asked my girlfriend (now my wife) if the college had changed

---

56. John Piper, *When I Don't Desire God: How to Fight for Joy* (Wheaton, IL: Crossway Books, 2004). Piper calls the believer to God in the midst of suffering as well as in times of prosperity. The joy in suffering is communicated here to show gladness as we are satisfied in Christ regardless of circumstance.

57. "Retinitis Pigmentosa," *Foundation Fighting Blindness,* accessed December 29, 2016, http://www.blindness.org/retinitis-pigmentosa. Retinitis Pigmentosa (RP) is a degenerative eye disease that strikes during adolescence and takes away night and peripheral vision and is usually followed by attacking central vision as well. Most people with RP are legally blind by age 40.

the bulbs recently. She confirmed they had not and this was the realization of the start of a very aggressive attack on my eyesight. Over the next seven years I would have cataract surgery, work temporarily at a sheltered workshop for the blind, adjust the settings on my computer multiple times, and creep my way through reading in seminary before finally being handed the final blow of blindness.

I still recall the flippant admonition of the doctor in 2003 when I was told for the first time I was "legally blind." I had never been to that particular office before, and I had a work-related physical checkup that assigned me there. As he walked out the door he said, "Well, you should be okay for at least another ten years of work and after that you should be good to go with getting Social Security since you are legally blind." The door shut, and I was sitting alone with the weight of this news. This struggle and fight has continued over the last decade and a half as I learn new technology and regain independence as abilities that were once mine slip from my grasp.

In 2012, as an urban missionary and church planter, I knew I had to get help. Like serious help. I was emotionally a wreck, and I had become exhausted from trying to hide my sight loss from anyone who surrounded me. Never asking anyone where the bathroom was proved miserable when I had to relieve myself. I was continually getting lost when trying to find new homes of Somali, Karen, and Bhutanese refugees new to the country. When I would ask the bus driver what number the bus was, they would treat me as if I were illiterate. I had no guide dog, no cane to identify my condition, and the general assumption was that I was fully sighted. Full acceptance of blindness had to happen if I would live a productive life.

That same year, I enrolled at a residential blindness adaptation program, BLIND, Inc. in Minneapolis and began to learn how to do things without sight. The philosophy of the program is to wear sleep shades at all times in order to learn how to function with total sight loss as vision fades. At the end of the six months, I had learned to travel anywhere with a cane independently, was a decent braille reader, and was able to perform all tasks on my phone and computer using special accessibility software. I mourned my losses so much in those days. The old life of vision was long gone, and I entered into a new life of permanently being labeled "blind" to the surrounding community. As difficult as it may seem, it was one of the best things that has ever happened to me.

The particular condition that I have is most evidenced by night blindness and for as long as I can remember I never did anything independently at night. The first time I took a solo trip from Minneapolis to St. Paul in the evening was sort of like floating on a cloud; I felt like I was flying. All the suffering and hard work was worth the freedom I was experiencing. Over and over again, my blindness has been used in ways I would have never imagined as I work with folks new to the country. Learning a foreign language, taking public transport, interacting in social situations—all these things take on new meaning as I interact and serve those in my neighborhood. When I put my arms around friends who have walked through hell and faced some of the most atrocious things imaginable, blindness creates this beautiful doorway to identify with them in their suffering. In human weakness, somehow the greatness of Christ is displayed in power.

The Beauty in the Losses of Karen Neighbors

Eh Paw is a dear Karen friend of mine from Burma who came to the US alone as a teenager about ten years ago. He basically lived in the jungle on the run from soldiers who were persecuting the Karen people of his country for most of his teen years. When he came to the US, he was staying in the Midwest somewhat isolated from the Karen community. One day a SWAT team showed up at his house and dragged him outside and threw him in the police car. With little English and no idea of what was happening, he was scared out of his mind. The police squad had made a mistake and had the wrong guy, but not before terrifying and reminding Eh Paw of the very hell that he had escaped from in Burma and Thailand.

When my wife and I met Eh Paw, the first thing we noticed about him was that his face glowed with the love of Jesus. Every single night it seemed we could find him reaching out and serving in practical ways for newly arrived Karen refugees. I don't think he ever slept. He was very involved at the small church I pastored in St. Paul, and on one of his visits he discovered that a young married couple was about to have their first child. The husband, Kaw, had fallen from a mango tree when he was eleven years old, and he now walked hunched over as he never got proper hospital treatment as a refugee in Thailand. Eh Paw discovered that Kaw was riding a ten-speed bike back and forth about seven miles to the hospital in subfreezing Minnesota temperatures to visit his wife who was having complications in her pregnancy.

Eh Paw told me about it and the next day about ten of us (most of our tiny organic church) showed up at the hospital and met Kaw and his wife Snie for the first time. That visit was a holy moment as all of Eh Paw's losses were being resurrected in

74

life-giving unity. Kaw and Snie became active members of our church, and they continually showed us the beautiful example of redemption. Eh Paw, Kaw, and Snie's lives are still extremely difficult. The road of the cross is one of sacrifice and suffering, but their story motivates so many to keep going.

Eh Paw will never be asked to speak at a major Christian conference on church planting or refugee ministry, but his servant's heart that has sprung from a life of deep pain and loss is invaluable. I will never forget his painful chuckle when he would be sitting on the hood of his car on summer nights in Minnesota sharing yet one more sacrifice he was forced to make along the refugee highway.[58] The lessons of suffering in up rootedness and transition have given Eh Paw a heart to willingly sacrifice for his community. Without much fanfare or strong family ties, Eh Paw is reflecting Jesus in suffering attempting to make Christ visible, not himself.[59]

---

58. To my knowledge the term "Refugee Highway" was coined by Tom Albinson, director of International Association for Refugees, several years ago. The term comes from the fact that there are well-worn paths across our globe that refugees travel to get to places of safety and desire to start a new life after being forced from their homeland. Further, Albinson reminds us that these paths are a scar on our globe of pain, up rootedness, and devastation. There are now domestic and international organizations with the same name in which Albinson is involved. See this website for more information: http://www.refugeehighway.net/.

59. Patrick Fung, "Live to be Forgotten Interview," *Urbana Missions Conference 2006,* accessed February 9, 2017, https://vimeo.com/8433862?lite=1. Fung challenges college students to live to be forgotten in a self-promotional age. Over the last decade I have returned to this video and passed it along to upcoming generations in cross-cultural work.

The Story of the City is a Story of Great Loss

For every person who resides in your neighborhood, there remains a story. Often there is deep loss in that story. A blind guy, a young man who spent his teen years roaming the jungles of Thailand and Burma, a mother of four who speaks little English and spent the previous twenty years in a refugee camp in eastern Nepal, an undocumented resident in Fresno or Chicago who works odd jobs because he doesn't have papers to obtain employment— these are stories of incredible loss. But these labels do not define us. We are not the disabled, the refugee, and the undocumented under the umbrella of the Kingdom. We are simply his children. Broken and scarred as we may be, we are simply people created in the image of Christ. As we look to Jesus, the suffering servant, we do not want to develop a labeling complex in urban mission.[60] We aren't trying to market our pain or the pain of our neighbors and sell it to mission donors.[61] Rather, we zoom-out to identify with our neighbors who have echoes of the Kingdom resounding through their losses. Let's capture his image as we discuss action steps, identifying with the scorn and shame of our Lord.

---

60. Eve Tuff, "Suspending Damage: A Letter to Communities," *Harvard Educational Review 79, no. 3 (Fall 2009): 413.*

61. Emily Roenigk, "5 Reasons 'Poverty Porn' Empowers the Wrong Person," *Huffington Post,* Apr 16, 2014, accessed December 28, 2016, http://www.huffingtonpost.com/emily-roenigk/poverty-charity-media_b_5155627.html. Roenigk writes that we often sell poverty to those in places of power rather than truly serve to empower those who most need it. This is obviously the opposite of our hopes.

Capture His Image

Talking openly about pain and suffering can be difficult. Oftentimes we can go to either extreme in magnifying our problems to be greater than they really are or minimizing them to the point where it is as if they do not exist. In my years of sitting with people around this theme, it tends to be the latter. We like to gloss over this as it can be difficult to discuss. Think about the Eh Paws in your neighborhood. Remember your neighbor who has endured incredible loss. You and those on your ministry team have all faced (perhaps you are facing right now) great pain. Dare to allow the Holy Spirit to penetrate this part of your journey and let him uncover pathways on how to reflect Jesus in suffering and sacrifice.

What losses are you presently dealing with emotionally, relationally, or physically? How has Christ identified with you in this struggle?

Who do you know who is suffering physically right now? Tell that story to the group and pray for him or her.

How can our physical disabilities or struggles draw us closer to Christ? How have you seen that in your life or in the life of someone you know?

Betrayal of those close to you, especially in the church cuts the heart like a knife. Ministry teams and church leadership struggle in maintaining healthy relationships as do all families. Further, the city seems to take no prisoners when it comes to abandonment and betrayal. Our tendency is to pull back as we fear the pain that will be endured along the way. To trust is to risk, and perhaps the Lord is calling us to start that journey. As you invite your ministry team and close neighbors into the conversation, listen to the voice of the Spirit as you capture his image together.

How can you relate to Jesus being betrayed by Judas? Are you still suffering the results of betrayal?

Do you feel like you have abandoned others at the point of their need? Describe that experience.

Jesus responded with confidence and grace as he was betrayed. What are some godly attitudes or daily practices you can take action on to follow this example better?

What steps can you take and encourage others to take when they are in the middle of betrayal? How do we lead others well who are in the dark cave of being forsaken?

Up rootedness is a narrative that is told throughout many urban areas. This story of war and loss may not be told to the average person on the street, but it is being told nonetheless. That narrative still remains extremely fresh on the minds and hearts of many of our neighbors. Years ago I recall Tom Albinson, World Evangelical Alliance Ambassador for Refugees, Displaced, and Stateless Peoples, saying that refugees and former refugees in our city have a story that they are dying to tell but no one ever asks about.[62] Think about your friends and neighbors who have been forced to migrate because of political, religious, or economic persecution. Perhaps you relocated due to such experience. Listen and discuss these questions with grace.

Tell your story of migration if you feel comfortable doing so. If no one is present with such a story, tell one or two stories of your friends who relocated to your city as a refugee.

What may be the greatest loss in all the moving, fighting, and process of starting over?

How does Christ on the cross speak to the story of uprootedness? How has Christ identified and how does he continue to identify with someone who has been forced to leave his country and start over again?

---

62. Tom Albinson leads walking tours in densely populated refugee neighborhoods where he encourages folks to keep their eyes and ears open as they engage with residents. Often conversations will happen around the uprootedness narrative if a person is patient enough to listen.

Pray for one or two people who come to mind who are having particular struggles with the suffering of uprootedness. Ask the Holy Spirit to give the joy and gladness of Jesus even in the midst of suffering.

Reflecting Christ in the midst of deep loss is one of the most challenging areas in surrendering to Jesus. We have to remind ourselves that we are not alone; our Master Servant also went through the loss that we face. He took on the weight of sin for all people and swallowed the bitter cup of shame in one gulp. We do follow in those footsteps, but we must remember that Jesus is not only a triumphant, ministry example to be followed; he is our Lord. No matter what the loss or how difficult the journey, we can run into his arms and find safety, healing, and redemption. As you close this chapter, ask God to fill you anew with his joy that is satisfied in every event and circumstance.

Chapter 4
REFLECTING HIS IMAGE IN DISCIPLESHIP

Zoom-In

"The time has come," he said. "The kingdom of God has come near. Repent and believe the good news!" (Mark 1:15)

"Come, follow me," Jesus said, "and I will send you out to fish for people." At once they left their nets and followed him. (Mark 1:17-18)

The Kingdom of God was the central message in the ministry of Jesus and roots the life of discipleship under his sovereign rule. Mark focuses belief and repentance around the reign of the Kingdom of God in Mark 1:14-15. Matthew 4:23 and Luke 4:43 also point to Jesus healing many kinds of diseases, preaching the Kingdom, and establishing this central message as the purpose of ministry. With such focus on the Kingdom of God, it is critical that Christlike ministry does not ignore such an invitation in discipleship.

The Kingdom of God

The first thing we find Jesus doing when inviting his disciples into a relationship is announcing the very Kingdom he had come to inaugurate. Both Old and New Testaments describe a kingdom that is not bound by territory or place but is the literal reign of God.[63] Contrasting the political topsy-turvy kingdoms of this world and unjust systems, Jesus invites the disciples into a Kingdom that has both already arrived yet not fully realized until its consummation at the end of the age.[64] This Kingdom is upside down when compared to the socio-political context of the disciples as well as the environment in our cities today. In Christ's Kingdom, the first are last (Matt. 20:16), the poor are rich (Matt. 5:3), outsiders become insiders (Mark 7:24-37), and the lost are found (Luke 15:1-10).[65]

When Jesus announced the arrival of the Kingdom, he was also pointing to an eventual consummation of such a Kingdom when all justice, mercy, and salvation will reign. God's intentions, his power, and his authority will be realized. As Jesus looks towards his first disciples and calls them to his Kingdom, this is obviously far more than religious dogma or creed. Jesus is calling the disciples into a Kingdom of power, righteousness, and blessedness that has just begun and will be fully understood in the future. At this point, the almighty reign of God will be complete, and its glory will be undeniable. Death is swallowed up; pain is annihilated; shame is defeated. The road of discipleship and

---

63. Robert Stein, Mark: Baker Exegetical Commentary on the New Testament, Kindle Location 2174.

64. Though there are differing views on the Kingdom of God and its coming, I use the "already, not yet" view as commonly referred to in theological and popular writing. The Kingdom of God is both a present reality among us as well as a future hope.

65. Donald Kraybill's The Upside-Down Kingdom refers to the nature of the Kingdom discussed at the close of this paragraph. Some of the paradoxes from Scripture are taken from this seminal work.

Kingdom pronouncement anticipates Christ's reign forever and ever.

The Kingdom of Power

Jesus was sent to the earth to destroy the works of the devil (1 John 3:8), and the Kingdom of God encapsulates this power. Ladd describes the power of the Kingdom well when he writes:

What is the Gospel of the Kingdom? What means the announcement that the Kingdom of God has come near? It is this—which God is now acting among men to deliver them from the bondage of Satan. It is the announcement that God in the person of Christ is doing something, if you please, is attacking the very kingdom of Satan himself. The exorcism of demons is proof that the Kingdom of God has come among men and is at work among them.[66]

The Kingdom to which Jesus calls disciples to is not simply a matter of talk but of power (1 Cor. 4:20) and takes a wartime posture.

Disease, sickness, demon-possession, even death itself can be evil powers that are overthrown by the might of God in God's kingdom. The model and example of Jesus displayed a life in the Kingdom that was characterized by God's power. Repentance and belief are critical to the discipleship process as we will study later, but the denial and refusal to introduce seekers to the strength of God is to not fully call disciples. Discipleship necessitates that we call people to the power of the Kingdom.

---

66. George Eldon Ladd, *The Gospel of the Kingdom* (1959; repr., The Paternoster Press, 2000), 46-47.

Our cities bring with them people caught in the grip of satanic bondage. Racism, unbelief, and habitual sin patterns rear their heads and set themselves up against the knowledge of God (2 Cor. 10:5). The power of the Kingdom must be present in the midst of such circumstances to overthrow such unbelief and evil. We all can name specific situations that describe far more than ignorance of diversity or neighbors who have made poor decisions; real evil powers are present but we are participants in a Kingdom of power that dispels the darkness.

The Righteousness of the Kingdom

Jesus said, "For I tell you that unless your righteousness surpasses that of the Pharisees and the teachers of the law, you will certainly not enter the kingdom of heaven" (Matt. 5:20). In Jesus' calling of the disciples, and thus when we call those in our city, we call people to a life of holiness. When Jesus addressed lust, anger, even giving generously, he zeroed in on the heart. In Mark 1, Jesus announced that the Kingdom of God had arrived, and this announcement was one of righteousness. In this Kingdom of righteousness, injustice is flipped on its head and the true holiness of God reigns.

Puritan Gurnall explains the righteousness of God as being both "imparted and imputed." This righteousness is something Christ does for and in the disciples. Christ imputes his righteousness, justifying us and making it possible for us to stand righteous before a holy God. Impartation is what Christ does in us, through the Spirit, to bring about righteous living in the world.[67]

---

67. William Gurnall, *The Christian in Complete Armour, vol. 2,* (Lindale, Texas: World Challenge Inc., 1988), 144-45.

Thus, when Jesus calls his first disciples into a discipling relationship, he is beckoning them to come into the Kingdom of righteousness. Transformation will bring about an imputed righteousness that only Christ can bring, and the ripple effects are the impartation of righteousness affecting every single thing we do in the world. The implications of Jesus' invitation to discipleship should transform or at least be transforming Christ's followers as well as every aspect of our lives as we live under his righteous reign.

The Time Has Come, Repent and Believe

This phrase "the time has come" is unique in that it implies an appointed time, an opportunity, an event, or perhaps a moment in time when everything changes.[68] The life of the Kingdom, as described in brief above, has dawned. Stein writes that this use of the word "time" (*kairos* as differentiated from *chronos* in Greek) is not so much pointing to an end of an old era but the arrival of the new.[69] Jesus is undoubtedly calling the disciples to a new era, a point in time where he is king and his Kingdom will rule in their hearts.

Jesus calls his disciples to the actions of repentance and obedience. Discipleship hinges on these two things. We can have all the other pieces aligned correctly—a beautiful invitation, an explanation of the Kingdom, the power of God overthrowing Satan with visible signs—but if repentance and belief are ignored, we completely miss the point of making disciples. Jesus calls his first disciples to repent and believe in Mark 1 thus announcing for

68. Mike Breen, *Building a Discipling Culture* (Pawleys Islands, SC: 3 Dimension Ministries, 2011), Kindle Location 703.

69. Stein, Kindle Location 2186.

people to turn from their sin and turn to God. This idea is synonymous with conversion, confessing that Jesus is Lord and choosing to now live in the ways of the Kingdom. Jesus did not select off the shelf, pre-packaged believers in choosing the disciples, but people who needed to turn to God, leave their sin, and believe in him.

Belief, as critical as it is to the discipleship process, should be put in proper balance with repentance in Jesus' Kingdom announcement. Scot McKnight stresses the priority in repentance when he argues that the coming of the Kingdom is a declaration that Jesus is King. Richard Beck in commentating on McKnight's *The King Jesus Gospel* writes: "Kings don't demand belief or faith. You don't believe in kings. No, you obey kings. You give a king allegiance. So when the Kingdom comes, the proper response is behavioral, a reconfiguration of loyalties."[70] If discipleship primarily focuses on what to believe and is void of obedience, the discipleship transformation will be short-circuited and incomplete. It is necessary to properly teach, just as Jesus modeled, that salvation has come. This salvation needs to be explained well having a strong focus towards repentance.

Come Follow Me

"Come, follow me," Jesus said, "and I will send you out to fish for people" (Matt. 4:19). In calling fishermen to leave their nets and follow him, Jesus' call of discipleship was radical. The chapters in the Gospels written after these events describe what

---

70. Richard Beck, "Repent The Kingdom Of Heaven Is At Hand: A Lenten Reflection," *Experimental Theology*, March 24, 2014, accessed January 26, 2017, http://experimentaltheology.blogspot.com/2014/03/repent-kingdom-of-heaven-is-at-hand.html.

following Jesus entails. Praying together, doing ministry, eating together, being sent out, fighting, watching Jesus do his miracles.

. . . the disciples were invited into the life of Jesus, and he modeled for them at every turn what a Kingdom life is supposed to be like. Christ seems to never miss an opportunity to teach, continually showing his coolness under the most tense of circumstances. The invitation to follow was an invitation into all areas of the life of Jesus. "You call me 'Teacher' and 'Lord,' and rightly so, for that is what I am" (John 13:13). Passing on information, theology, and turning every opportunity into a classroom permeated Christ's ministry. Ferdinando delineates the intent Jesus had in seeking, calling, training, and releasing in his ministry. He uses the language of apprentice training with an exact vocational goal.[71] As the disciples repented, they entered into believing and that belief would eventually equip them to make more disciples.

The first call to be disciples that Jesus made was also an invitation into making more disciples. Jesus said that he would teach these initial followers to "fish for people." In the short time the Twelve had together, Jesus prepares them to do this. He prepares them in such a way that even after all leave him during the crucifixion, Jesus still has enough trust in them to leave the entire future of the Church in their hands. When he commissions them to go and make disciples in Matthew 28, a reader would wonder why Jesus had so much trust. He prepared his disciples well. They spent hundreds of hours with Jesus. He knew them

---

71. Keith Ferdinando, "Jesus the Theological Educator," *Themelious* 38, no. 3 (November 2013), accessed January 26, 2017, http://themelios.thegospelcoalition.org/article/jesus-the-theological-educator.

inside and out. It is no question why the disciples in Acts were able to lead a revolution unlike the world has ever seen.

Zoom-Out

"Making disciples" is the mission that Jesus left in the hands of his followers and is our God-given responsibility. Innumerable resources have been written on the topic over the years in an attempt to accurately reflect the image of Christ. Colloquially and academically, we often mean very different things when we discuss such a term.[72] Urban ministry often stirs thoughts and strategies of living in close proximity of neighbors, sharing all aspects of our lives. This can at times be disconnected from the discipleship process. While this may be unintentional, it would still seem prudent to closely align the intensity of living in the city with the forming of disciples of Jesus.

When Neighbors Call the Bluff on Your Discipleship Ministry

Santosh is pretty much on his own and lives across the street from us. You met him in the previous chapter when he shared his thoughts on prayer. Just last week, he found out that his father and stepmother missed the cutoff date to be resettled as refugees in the United States and will apply for resettlement in Australia. This was after a four-and-a-half years wait with high hopes that they would live together once they were reunited in

---

72. Timothy Keller, *Loving the City: Doing Gospel-Centered Ministry in Your City* (Grand Rapids, MI: Zondervan Publishing, 2016), 242-250. Keller delineates the various views and approaches believers have in engaging culture in the discipleship process, asserting that all the views are both right and wrong. There are innumerable opinions on engaging culture in discipleship.

America.[73] Not so. Santosh knows every detail about my life and I know his. Several times throughout the week he stops by at our place, and it seems he almost always has a perplexing question about the gospel, an inquiry to defeat sin in his life, or how to better practice Christian unity in the body of Christ. Our conversations can go for hours. This is an urban missionary's dream, but I have noticed myself getting antsy at times when I'm just not spiritually alert enough or full of God enough to continue discipling Santosh. It is the most intense discipling relationship I have had in fifteen years of ministry.

About three months ago, Santosh and I were talking about the relationship we had and I began to weep as I described how deeply he has blessed me in friendship and discipleship. I looked across our kitchen table and said, "Santosh, you don't let me be lazy. You just don't allow me to clock-in or clock-out when it comes to my walk with Christ. You challenge me in so many ways, and I have grown more in the last year with you than at any other time in my life. There are days when I just don't want to pray with you, or study the Bible, or answer some theological question. But this is a gift that I have been given. I never want to take this relationship for granted. This is what anyone who loves Jesus would dream for his life—to be discipled in addition to helping a friend grow in discipleship." Santosh returned the encouragement and confession with such appreciation and compassion.

It was a holy moment. These moments happen often with Santosh, but it is not a walk in the park. We get mad at each other

---

73. Both the Bhutanese-Nepali culture of not saying something will happen until it has in fact taken place combined with the uncertainty of resettlement kept Santosh in flux. This uncertainty, culturally and situationally, leaves many with little control in the resettlement process.

sometimes. We disagree. We laugh. We cry. I have sat in my basement listening to the aftermath of horrible decisions Santosh has made. He has picked me up when I've gone off the rails. We have access to each other's life and that kind of access means that we share most details of life together. Santosh has called the bluff on my Christianity over and over again. I don't get to decide when I'm on or when I'm off when it comes to discipleship. Every day at any moment is a moment to announce the Kingdom.

Discipleship in the Lowell Neighborhood

The Lowell neighborhood of Fresno is a place that most people tend to avoid. Nancy has chosen to make this place home and has discipled many young people during her time there. The longevity in the community has allowed Nancy to be able to be present during the most momentous and devastating times of the lives of her neighbors. Nancy is a nurse and recently she missed a work meeting we had because she rushed to the hospital to be with a young girl named Naomi who was having complications during childbirth. She had watched Naomi grow up and now was able to demonstrate afresh what it means to be present in moments of distress and joy.

Last month found Nancy at a nearby prison. She ran into two young men from the neighborhood that she had forgotten were incarcerated. Both of them gave her thanks for the life she has lived with them in community. A month or two prior to that, another kid in Nancy's youth group returned to Lowell after being in the military and has signed on to her missions organization to join in full-time work in the inner city. From the hospital, to the prison, and back to the sanctuary, Nancy has stayed faithful to the laborious task of making disciples. Unconventional as some of these forms or situations may be throughout the discipleship process, Nancy keeps her hand to the plow and does not look back.

In February of 2017, Nancy was reflecting on the task of forming disciples and seeing folks from her neighborhood raised up into ministry. I was on a conference call with her in which several of us were trying to figure out how to mobilize ethnic leaders who likely did not have the financial capital to fundraise in urban ministry. The call took an interesting turn when someone asked whether or not our ministries needed to be in our neighborhoods. What was our legitimacy there? When it came time for Nancy to speak she giggled her Valley girl laugh and said, "Here is a novel idea. Maybe it is not so much about our urban neighbors needing us, but us needing them."[74] Silence filled the conversation. And that sort of commitment and deep value in the lives of those in Lowell is what enables long-term, transformative discipling relationships.

Discipling Undocumented Young Men in Chicago

Chris and Krista Ophus work with a Mexican community wherein many of its residents are undocumented. While Krista slips away to teach at a neighborhood school, Chris finds himself getting his hands into all kinds of activities that the typical pastor wouldn't think to do. Meeting with young men who are away from their families in Mexico during the day because they work all night

---

74. Jonathan Brooks, "I'm Here Because You're Here" in *Making Neighborhoods Whole* by Wayne Gordons and John Perkins (Downers Grove, IL: IVP, 2013), 64-70. The notion of needing our neighbors as much as they need us is a guiding principle of CCDA and many urban ministries around the world. Brooks shares of an incident that took his family from avoiding neighbors to needing them as the people in the house next door were shot and paramedics were called. Undoubtedly, Nancy has been impacted by very similar incidences.

filled Chris's schedule in the early years in the neighborhood. Temptations with sexual sin, loneliness, trying to earn a fair wage—these were all issues that Chris tackled as he discipled the men in his community.

Chris's friend and pastor of New Life Community Church, Paco, once said that the problem with Chris is that everyone thinks Chris is his best friend. "I think he is my best friend, but then I turn around and he is some other guy's best friend. This is just the kind of reputation he has in Little Village." He went on to say that Chris could use his white skin to represent people in ways that he could not. He smiled as he shared about Chris getting all dressed up in a suit and carrying a briefcase to represent men in court.[75] Chris was not merely a translator but his knowledge of the legal system, ability to walk in both worlds, and a compassion to disciple them through every detail of life make an incredible difference.

Paco and Chris disciple one another in ways that each of them never dreamed, growing up with a very different set of circumstances. Chris and Paco's friendship is a daily lesson on what discipleship means in a complex immigrant neighborhood in America. Reflecting Jesus in the city calls for discipling friendships and practices that are far outside the lines of what many of us traditionally consider spiritual formation.

Discipleship in the Karen Community in Minneapolis-St. Paul

Many in the Karen community have been through terrible horrors that need not be repeated. Saw Paw came to Minnesota in

---

75. Paco Amador, "Urban Issues in Ministry" (presentation, International Teams US Area Leaders, Elgin, Illinois, May 2-6, 2015).

2009 with his wife and two young children. I met them the first day they were in the country. I walked into their apartment, and it was a disaster. The oven and stove were full of rust and had not been used in months. Cockroaches were everywhere. There was a stench in the building that never went away. Saw helped me clean the stove that night though he was exhausted from his long flight from Thailand. I am confident he had no idea why we were cleaning such a machine if we were just going to get it dirty with fire again, but he served nevertheless.

Less than a week later and no more than two weeks after they had arrived in the country, I walked into the apartment and found about twenty children singing action Bible kids songs. They were all in unison, and as I popped through the door Saw said in his limited English, "Sunday school for kids." I came to find out that Saw was running kids programs a few days a week in his apartment, and people were meeting frequently to pray and study the Bible together. It was not uncommon for ten to twelve people to come in and out of Saw Paw's apartment when I would visit.

He did not need a title or invitation to begin discipleship. Saw Paw simply met some of his new Karen neighbors and got to work.

Thomas and Kathy Ritnorakan also live in the Karen community in St. Paul, MN, and have modeled what it means to follow Jesus and call others to do the same. They now pastor a church that has grown to more than 200 members, and most of the growth has happened from them single-handedly inviting people into their lives. Kathy has ladies struggling through new life in America come sleep at her house, and Thomas spends countless hours helping in practical ways with community members. This blending of trying to help folks make it in a new country and intense spiritual discipleship is a task that few are willing to attempt. Though they have no Bible school degrees behind their names, they are modeling and teaching about the Jesus they know and follow. Extreme access to their lives, vulnerability, and release into service are the cries of their hearts.

Models and Discipleship Training Overload

I have no qualms about using curriculum or taking discipleship models and implementing them into our urban ministries. Many have gone before us and developed rich, well-suited material that facilitates great disciple multiplication. The challenge, however, is making sure our emphasis rests on the life and work of Jesus and not on the current method we are using. There is no doubt in my mind that many indigenous leaders are doing exceptionally well in some areas of the discipleship process and failing in others. If all of us in our contemporary settings were honest, we too must admit mistakes we are making.

Using the example of Christ as a basis for discipleship necessitates full access into one another's life. Teaching is required. Learning. Growing. Modeling. Releasing. Multiplying. All of those things are critical to our ministry. They all happen, however, in the context of relationship and extravagant time invested with others. Discipleship must be rooted deeply in Scripture and ooze out into the contexts in which we find ourselves. May we catch the heart and example of Jesus in discipleship as we reflect him in the city.

Capture His Image

The urban context is a place that has often been hostile to people. Many have come to the city in search of a better life, and they were delivered just the opposite. Those from refugee and immigrant backgrounds have been victims of torture, war, and broken government systems. People have come and gone in the lives of so many in our neighborhoods. Why then would we think that an invitation into discipleship will make much of a difference? Why would anyone listen?

We must remember that the Kingdom to which we are inviting people into is the Kingdom of power, the Kingdom of righteousness, and a Kingdom that flips all other life upside down. This Kingdom knows no end and as we announce God's Kingdom, we can expect his fullness and life to be present. We can expect the very life that Jesus brings to be present even in the direst of circumstances. Discipleship though is a marathon. It is not for those who give up easily. Christ has invited us into his Kingdom and has called us to hang in there for the long haul with people. Let us discuss and reflect together what a life in the Kingdom entails and how discipleship is developing in your community.

What are you or your ministry currently doing to make disciples?

Are you inviting followers into a Kingdom of power and righteousness? How so?

What aspects of the Kingdom in this chapter do you struggle with the most? What are some steps to improve going forward?

What are some areas that those whom you are discipling need to be strengthened in?

The previous questions are designed to get us thinking about the Kingdom of God and discipleship as outlined in the Gospel, particularly when Christ called disciples to repent and believe. Sometimes we can worry so much about the practical implications of discipleship (e.g. what curriculum to use, where to meet, who is going to be in a discipleship group, etc.) that we neglect the weightier matters of making disciples in the city. Let us look more on the following Jesus and modeling piece as we seek to capture his image.

Briefly describe your discipleship story. Who discipled you and what did that entail?

How accessible are you to those you are discipling?

Are you and those you are discipling holding each other accountable in areas in which you struggle? Are you praying together?

How much time are you spending with them? Would they say you are accessible as well?

What are you doing with those you are discipling to teach them how to serve and minister? Are you serving together?

What fun things are you and your disciples doing together not directly related to ministry?

Let's take a moment to think about passing the gospel on to the next generation or those whom you are training. To speak in generalities always gets us off the hook in terms of the kinds of actions we put into practice. If we are not intentional, we will let this glorious gospel roll off our lips and be heard in the ears hundreds of times by those in our neighborhoods, but if we fail to call to repentance and direct obedience, the multiplication of disciples will not happen. Write down four or five names of people you are discipling right now. Answer the following questions about the names on your list.

If John (say the name of each person on your list) was completely left without me, could he make disciples? Why or why not?

How do I need to invite each of these people into my life in more intentional ways that reflect your Kingdom? How do I need to challenge them?

Has anyone on your list shared the gospel with someone in the last six months? Are they currently discipling anyone that you know of?

Consider meeting weekly with the people on your list once a week for the next year (maybe you are already doing so). What fears or challenges would this intense of a discipling relationship involve?

Pray for each other in your study group to patiently, yet intensely make disciples in your city.

Discipleship is the task of every Christ-follower, and we never outgrow our need for it. The incarnation of Christ showed a patient yet intense life with his followers. The time they all spent together unarguably knit them together and transformed them to reflect God much more clearly. The end result is beautiful but the process of growing and developing is one of the more painful parts of the Christian experience. The demand of discipleship, however, calls for the same patient intensity that Christ gave to his disciples.

All who have worked in the city have received a text late into the evening where a crisis has just happened. Sitting with neighbors in your living room as they weep over ongoing struggles in their lives is not uncommon. Our homes have become sanctuaries, and we don't exactly get to schedule when the Kingdom of God will come. In order to truly capture the image of Jesus in discipleship, we must be spiritually alert, patient, and continually listening to the Spirit's voice. May we all continue to shine Christ's image in the darkness so brightly that our neighborhoods will repent and believe the Good News.

Chapter 5
REFLECTING HIS IMAGE IN COMPASSION

Zoom-In

Jesus went through all the towns and villages, teaching in their synagogues, proclaiming the good news of the kingdom and healing every disease and sickness. When he saw the crowds, he had compassion on them, because they were harassed and helpless, like sheep without a shepherd. Then he said to his disciples, "The harvest is plentiful but the workers are few. Ask the Lord of the harvest, therefore, to send out workers into his harvest field." (Matt. 9:35-38)

Acts of compassion and mercy become a theme throughout the life and ministry of Jesus as read in the Gospels. Despite the severity and importance of the mission before him, Christ continually reaches out in compassion to those in great need. The Good Shepherd can be found suffering with the most unlikely of people. In Mark 1:40-41, Christ reaches out, touches, and heals a man with leprosy. He heals a widow's son by raising him from the dead (Luke 7:13-15); he heals two blind men (Matt. 20:34); he has compassion on the crowd of 5,000 who had gathered and had no food (Mark 8:2); he talks with the woman at the well and woman caught in adultery (John 4; 8:1-11); and he tells the Parable of the Good Samaritan explaining that we must show compassion to those in distress (Luke 10:25-37).

The list keeps going as Jesus heals dozens of diseases, spends time with tax collectors and sinners, and defies the culture of the day by touching others many would not touch. For Christ, acts of compassion were not a ministry to be done but a life to be lived. In choosing to empty himself and incarnate the Word of God, Jesus lived among and suffered with those in the cities, towns, and villages.

Suffering with People

Compassion combines the two words *passion* and *with*, literally translated "suffering with."[76] Several commentators point to the feeling that you have deep in your gut, in the bowels of a person when it comes to the emotion of deep compassion. Blomberg expounds on this gut-level compassion in Matthew 9 as being one that looks to the crowds and realizing that there are no leaders to lead them. They truly are harassed and helpless and need someone to suffer with them in order to be found.[77] It is further worth noting that this compassion, the suffering with that we see in the life of Jesus, combines both personal interaction and biblical teaching on what it means to live a compassionate life.[78]

---

76. G. Walter Hansen, "The Emotions of Jesus," *Christianity Today,* February 3, 1997, accessed February 10, 2017, http://www.christianitytoday.com/ct/1997/february3/7t2042.html.

77. Craig L. Blomberg, *The New American Commentary,* vol. 22, *Matthew* (Holman, 1992), 166.

78. Wayne Jackson, "The Compassion of Christ," in *Christian Courier,* accessed February 10, 2017, https://www.christiancourier.com/articles/947-compassion-of-christ-the. The author discusses how Jesus shows very clearly that he is compassionate in how he relates to others. He further illuminates this in his teaching in the parables of the lost coin, lost sheep, lost son, and even in reaching out to the Samaritan on the side of the road.

Again, these decisions to both teach and live out compassion in personal relationships are no mere ministry strategy. Nouwen and co-authors make the strong point in their book on compassion that this lifestyle is the very nature of the incarnation itself.[79] The self-emptying of Christ is an act of compassion. This act displays to the world that Christ is not only coming to the world to help the oppressed and the poor. Rather, Christ himself becomes poor, becomes oppressed, and endures suffering to the point of the cross. In every possible way Jesus is our compassionate servant. This has major implications for how we choose to live and work in the city. If Christ himself felt that he had no right to power or luxury (Phil. 2), should not the urban worker also emulate this example? Christ emptied himself, suffered with those all around him, entered into their lives, and brought the compassionate love of God that came from his Father.

Compassion Translates to the Calling Out and Sending of Workers

Jesus saw the crowds and his compassion instructs his followers to pray for workers. This Scripture from Matthew 9 becomes both a prayer and a commission. As illuminated in chapter two, on reflecting Jesus in prayer, the call to reflect Jesus in the city is a call to prayer. A call to prayer is a call to action. In the compassion of Jesus amongst the crowds, there is an

---

79. Henri Nouwen, Donald McNeill, and Douglas Morrison, *Compassion: A Reflection on the Christian Life,* rev. ed. (Image Publishers, 2006). Nouwen, McNeill, and Morrison outline the depths of a compassionate life for the Christian, delineating the process it was for Christ to enter into this life. Notable is the choice Christ made to become poor, human, and shamed himself rather than merely showing compassion on those who were shamed, poor, or walked in humanity. Compassion is connected well to the incarnation here.

assumption that the harvest field needs workers. It is the responsibility of disciples to both pray and work hard, displaying Christ's compassion to those who are harassed and helpless, those who are like sheep without a shepherd.

Matthew chose to write from a very distinct vantage point that helps us see Jesus as a compassionate servant and king. In seeing those whom most of the world sees as invisible, the instructions to pray and go are critical. Carr, a scholar on Dalit theology, expounds upon the context of Matthew 9. The crowds and the migrants gathered in the city, who are far removed from their homelands, will be the very people to bring about compassion once redeemed.

Matthew sought to portray Jesus as the Shepherd-King differently from the way in which he was expected to gather together the Diaspora and lead them home. The Shepherd-King of Matthew, namely Jesus, did indeed gather together the lost sheep of the House of Israel. However, the identity of the lost sheep of the house of Israel was now redefined. They were not the ethnic Israel comfortably settled among the nations. They were, in fact, the despised Galileans, exploited poor, physically handicapped that were deemed cursed, hated tax gatherers, and stigmatized women sex workers. They were the lost sheep of the House of Israel and they were the poor in Spirit who were to inherit God's kingdom (Matt. 5:3). Jesus gathered these socially and culturally scattered people together and gave them community status. Their sense of dignity was restored. Above all, as the collective who would inherit God's kingdom, they were given charge of the mission to the nations.[80]

Jesus sees the crowds and has compassion. He calls out workers. Undoubtedly the very gospel project is going to be left in the hands of the ones to whom Jesus extends his compassion. In our cities, we too will be surrounded by the seekers of our urban neighborhoods. The Lord of the harvest will respond to our cries for workers in urban centers. People stumbling to find their way spiritually, physically, and emotionally cross our paths. The compassionate example of Jesus calls for us to both see people, enter into their stories, and pray for more workers to live among them thus having transformed communities.

Suffering and Joy Together

Patrick Fung, director of OMF International, was interviewed some years ago at Urbana's mission conference for college students. He highlighted taking risks for God, trusting in God to provide, and living a life to be forgotten so that Christ would be remembered. He emphasizes the point that suffering and joy are always compatible.[81] Understanding that compassion requires suffering with those we serve, there must be strength in joy as we live out compassion. Fung further comments that bitterness is never compatible with compassionate suffering.

Jesus displays this kind of compassion throughout his life and ministry. Philippians 2, a text foundational to Christlikeness, admonishes us to make our joy complete by walking with others in

---

80. Dhyanchand Carr, "Jesus' Identification with Galilee and Dalit Hermeneutic," accessed February 9, 2017, http://cca.org.hk/home/ctc/ctc03-03/ctc03-03b.htm.

81. Fung, "Live to be Forgotten Interview."

unity and love while ultimately having the attitude of Christ. This attitude was one of compassion and joy wherein Jesus did not consider himself entitled. He became a servant and showed compassion to all. Philippians further expounds the joy of the Lord being our strength (Phil. 4:4), even in suffering. This joy is a supernatural work of the Spirit that comes from abiding in Christ. Hebrews 12:2 paints the undeniable picture of a life of compassion where Christ gives his perfect, sinless life for those who were harassed and helpless. "For the joy set before him he endured the cross, scorning its shame . . ." This is the joyous compassion of Jesus that must be reflected in our cities.

The Self-Emptying of Christ in Compassion

John 1 and Philippians 2 emphasize the incarnation of Christ as central themes in the gospel. It is certainly true that redemption would not be possible without incarnation. This self-emptying or *kenosis,* as it is referred to in theological circles, focuses heavily on what Christ gave up in coming to earth.[82] His omniscience, his glory, and his equality with God were laid down and displayed through surrender. Byrd, however, emphasizes what Christ entered into which is critical to our discussion. Indeed, he did set aside many things, but Christ took on humanity.[83] That humanity is what made it possible for Christ to set an example and identify with the world thus giving salvation to all in the most paradoxical way imaginable.

---

82. David T. Williams, *Kenosis of God* (iUniverse, 2009).

83. Michael F. Byrd, *Evangelical Theology: A Biblical and Systematic Introduction* (Grand Rapids, MI: Zondervan, 2013), Kindle Location 10544-47.

The taking on of humanity that John refers to as "tabernacling, pitching his tent" among us is what grants access into the lives of people. We would never know the deep, beloved compassion of Jesus without entering into that humanity. Reminding us that the incarnational model for urban ministry is not perfect, this is still a necessary reminder for us. Yes, we are not the Messiah. We cannot nor should not reincarnate God becoming man. Nonetheless, his image is beautiful. Christ enters into the lives of people. He laughs, cries, dines, prays, and suffers with people. Compassion flows out of a life fully given to his friends and community.

Zooming-in on the biblical text is a call to see the crowds. It is a call to those on the margins of society. It is a call to pray for workers in our neighborhoods. Undeniably, we will make practical choices in regard to life and ministry—where to live, what schools our kids should attend, what outreaches to initiate. These, however, cannot be the initial decisions in reflecting Jesus in the city. The call of Scripture is to reflect the compassionate nature of Jesus which permeated everything he said and did.

Zoom-Out

"John, can you tell me about the process of getting a gun? Is it difficult?" I paused nervously and responded. Purna had been in the country less than two months and was riddled with questions.

"Why do you want a gun?" I asked.

"Well, it has happened two times now. My relatives in Minneapolis are being harassed because they are new. Some gang members or some sort of rough guys see them in front of their house and follow them. My uncle was beaten up and had to go to the hospital because of that. Another member of the family was on the bus the other day, and someone asked my nephew a question. He did not know how to respond in English. The man started laughing and slapped him in the face really hard and then ran off the bus."

Again, I paused, looking for the right words in response to the events. I assured my friend that there was a process of getting a gun, but I mentioned how troublesome it could be in a crowded city like ours. If something were to happen and his relatives could not communicate what happened exactly, they could go to prison for a long time. Purna mentioned that they had called the police but when the police came, there was no translator, and they did not believe the events that had transpired. I sat in silence with my friends who were being beaten down, harassed, and somewhat helpless in a new land that they were still trying to navigate.

Compassion, to be with someone in their suffering, is challenging at any level. How much greater the need is when this involves people in our neighborhoods who are literally invisible to the surrounding community. The Bhutanese-Nepali began to be resettled to the US in 2008 during the economic recession, and jobs were difficult to find. In the midst of racism and injustice as we saw with Purna, people were left to obtain employment, learn language, and adjust to a country whose cultural distance is about as far away as it could possibly be. In those early days of resettlement, it was common for Bhutanese to tell me, "Everything is different here. The roads are different. Language is different.

Schools. Laws. Rules. Everything is different here."[84] To that massive adjustment, the church in the city is often blind. It seems that those who are geographically close to these realities somehow don't see the changes as they are taking place.[85] Churches in the suburbs often hear or read about the changes and want to drive into the city to do something. They don't have the time, commitment, nor trust to enter into this life for new neighbors. The kind of compassion that is needed is often overlooked.

Small Church with Big Compassion

In 2010, Pastor Dan Cramer of Zion Christian Church in Pittsburgh saw the Bhutanese-Nepali influx drastically changing his urban neighborhood. His church sat along the busiest street in the Carrick community of south Pittsburgh for years, but suddenly there was a surge of residents that he had not seen before. Jewish Family Services, a local resettling agency, asked if they could use space at one of the church's buildings for operating refugee services. He agreed. Dan wanted to do something though. He wanted his church to do something. With deep compassion in his heart, he began visiting new families one by one at an apartment

---

84. Om Dhungana, the second Bhutanese-Nepali man I ever met, introduced me to the phrase "everything is different here." That perspective has been echoed by hundreds of Nepalis throughout Minneapolis and Pittsburgh over the last decade.

85. Ralph D. Winter and Bruce A. Koch, "Finishing the Task: The Unreached People Challenge" in *Perspectives on the World Christian Movement: A Reader, 3rd* ed. (Pasadena, CA: William Carey Library Pub., 1974). Winter focuses on unreached people groups and barriers to the gospel. People blindness refers to those who are unable to see or engage neighbors in their own geographical area because of issues of racism, cultural, or societal ignorance. In other words, we ignore entire populations of people because we are blind to the fact that they remain around us. This is the story for many immigrant communities in America. Proximity often means ignoring.

complex next to the church. This complex would eventually become 95% Nepali providing a tremendous on-ramp into relationship building with new neighbors. With his hours of investment, weeks turned into months, and now months have turned into seven years of compassionate presence in the lives of his new neighbors.[86]

Pastor Dan was in his late fifties when this all began to take place, but he made a commitment to dig his heels in the ground and offer compassion in Jesus' name. Now, everyone in the Bhutanese community knows him as he walks up and down Brownsville Road, the community's main corridor. They know he is a Christian; he knows they are Hindu. Still he stays present in their lives by giving much of his time to the changing community. Currently, the Sunday school at Zion Christian Church is 90% Bhutanese-Nepali, and a group of committed teachers and assistants educate over forty Hindu background kids every week. Zion has partnered with YWAM to run a Wednesday youth group wherein twenty plus teens gather who are almost all from Hindu backgrounds. An ESL program has been started at the church, and the city's largest food pantry runs monthly out of Zion.[87] Dozens of Nepali folks get their practical needs met in this way.

This kind of compassion doesn't make sense in the eyes of the world, but it has been Pastor Dan's commitment to the compassion of Jesus that fuels involvement. Another congregant, a woman in her early fifties, is a professional dance teacher and has

86. Dan Cramer, "Mission in Smaller Churches," Catalyst Services, October 2014, accessed February 10, 2017, http://catalystservices.org/wp-content/uploads/2014/10/Missions-in-Smaller-Churches.pdf.

87. Zion Christian Church, "Networking in Missions," accessed April 17, 2017, http://zioncc.org/connection-points/networking-in-missions.

been doing dance classes for children and youth at Zion. Initiatives continue to mushroom and influence grows. Zion has become a trusted ministry of compassion in their neighborhood. Language barriers abound. Communication with adults is extremely limited. Still, the compassion of Christ compels them to do something that will make a difference for all eternity.

Compassionate Ministry in Chicago

"That's the hard part of doing gang intervention," Jorge says. "Going to the hospital and hearing the mom say through her tears, 'He didn't make it'; there is pain. There is emptiness. It is heart-breaking."[88]

Jorge and Benny grew up gang-banging on the opposite sides of Little Village adrift imaginary gang borders. The community is known for its gang wars, and many young people lose their lives. In a recent *Chicago Tribune* interview Benny commented, "It is not just kids involved in gangs getting killed but kids just walking who are not in gangs . . . we're losing young men not just to violence, but to prison."[89] You can hear the brokenness in the voices of Benny and Jorge who now work at New Life Community Church's Urban Skills Program. Urban Skills works with guys who are on probation or parole, and they are mandated by the courts to go through the program. This unlikely pair, Jorge and Benny, are united under Christ and have given two decades

---

88. Peter Nickeas, E. Jason Wambsgans, and Mary Schmich, "Benny and Jorge and the Quest for Peace in Little Village, *Chicago Tribune*, May 1, 2017, accessed June 1, 2017, http://www.chicagotribune.com/news/peacemakers/ct-little-village-met-20170421-story.html.

89. Ibid.

now to helping kids get off the streets. Jorge said of Benny when they sat down together, "He is unconditional; he loves people when they are at their worst."[90]

New Life Community Church and the Urban Life Skills initiative to serve gang members is a contemporary display of exemplary compassion in the face of overwhelming need. Literally, people's lives are at stake—children lose fathers, mothers lose their sons, and siblings lose their brothers. A certain percentage of gang members coast through the program but still return to the hellish life they knew before.[91] For many though, Jorge, Benny, and numerous others are mentoring young men and their families through some of the darkest days they have ever known. For Little Village and many who reside there, this is the compassion of Jesus reflected in the most visible way imaginable.

The city presents tremendous challenges. We cannot right all the wrongs taking place, but if we are going to follow Jesus' example, a compassionate response is demanded. To go further, we need a compassionate lifestyle that shows our neighbors in Word and deed that Jesus Christ has come. It is common for those working in urban ministry to get compassion fatigue and burn out.[92] The challenge of the city has to be put in proper perspective with prayer, rest, commitment, and love.

---

90. Ibid.

91. Urban Life Skills, accessed April 30, 2017, https://newlifecenters.org/our-programs/urban-life-skills/. Of the participants, 60% complete the Urban Life Skills program and do not offend again. A total of 71% successfully graduate the program.

92. Susanne Babble, "Compassion Fatigue," *Psychology Today,* July 4, 2012, accessed February 8, 2017, https://www.psychologytoday.com/blog/somatic-psychology/201207/compassion-

Throughout Scripture, God has a special place in his heart for the stranger, the widow, and the orphan. Jesus too spends a good portion of his ministry among those who are being overlooked by the broader population. The woman at the well, prostitutes, the choosing of disciples who were religiously unqualified, the disabled—Jesus cares for those who seem invisible. This piece of the incarnation is not merely an add-on but an integral part of what it meant that the Messiah had come. Remember the opening chapter on the very mission of Christ. Jesus came to bring freedom to those in the face of oppression and to announce the Good News. As we spend time assessing how to respond to the biblical text, may we remember the compassionate nature of Christ and internalize such an image in our hearts that results in Spirit-directed, righteous deeds.

---

fatigue. Those working in environments with those who have experienced trauma often take on the weight of the suffering of their clients. Upwards of 90% of workers admit to being exhausted from the compassion they extend. These findings not only reflect a secular audience but also research findings in Christian ministry among communities of great need as well.

Capture His Image

Our response to the Spirit to reflect the image of Jesus in compassion will largely indicate to what degree of integrity the gospel will have in our cities. Non-profits and organizational initiatives abound with paid workers performing social aid. City dwellers know this. While many in the urban centers will be appreciative of such programs, the example of Christ's compassion demands more than a programmatic response. Jesus emptied himself, became poor, moved into the neighborhood, and suffered with those whom most in the broader society did not want to touch. This compassionate Servant-King led with humility and power while entering into the suffering of the people around him.

Such compassion sprang from the joy of God and was evidenced in Christ's life and work. We too are entering into the suffering of the city. In some ways we are leaving certain rights or privileges behind.[93] We have been so transformed that we now see things from a completely different perspective. We look at the crowds, our neighbors . . . the refugee, the orphan, the poor. We see them. We know them by name. We share our life with them. Labels such as the ones I've just mentioned on the marginalized of our day fall away. Strangers have become friends as we share lives of compassion together.

We are not there yet, however. There are many lessons to be learned and issues to plow through. Let us discuss together what exactly it may take to reflect the compassion of Jesus in the city. Answer honestly and challenge one another with follow-up questions.

---

93. Mabel Williamson, *Have We No Rights?: A Frank Discussion of the "Rights" of Missionaries*, rev. ed., (Chicago, Moody Press, 2011).

Who is the widow, orphan, and refugee in your community?

Do political, government, or education leaders know who is invisible in your community? Have you talked with any of these leaders or heard their opinions of such people?

After reading this chapter, what do you feel the Spirit may be asking you to give up in order to walk in compassion with your neighbors?

Think about your own background and upbringing. What are some ways you have personally felt vulnerable and invisible? How may God use this in the city?

So much of staying alert in urban mission is getting out of bed and showing up. A colleague I know in Chicago has termed this, "the theology of hanging around."[94] Sometimes you just simply have to be there but if we never see people, we will never

---

94. Mark Soderquist, former Director of Urban Ministries for International Teams and resident in the Lawndale neighborhood of Chicago for the last three decades, often remarks that simply being present and available is one of the most essential pieces in urban mission. He calls it "the theology of hanging around."

engage. People in our cities are incredibly busy, and we can get sucked into the typical American mindset that our lives should be kept private, and people don't need to be bothered. We can also choose the Jesus road. Perhaps the Lord is asking us to suffer with others and to allow his joy to fill our streets.

Let's reflect a bit more on Scripture and discuss some of the people and situations God used to announce his Kingdom of compassion. We have briefly cited some of those examples throughout this book.

Who are some of the men and women throughout Scripture who seem like unlikely people to step into God's mission? How or why do you believe they overcame the odds stacked against them?

Choose one of the stories or examples of compassion in the life of Jesus. Why do you find this story so meaningful when you think about a life of compassionate mission in the city?

How are doing compassionate acts in Jesus' name the same or different from living a compassionate mission?

What changes do you need to make in your present ministry in order for your organization to be characterized by compassion?

Holistic mission is a very catchy phrase these days. Oftentimes young people and ministries who desire to stay current like to use as much lingo as they can to stay relevant. *Holistic ministry,* with strong implications of living amongst those you serve, has become such a term. When people are in their early twenties, it seems really cool to sell everything and live in the city. When you are forty and have three kids in school, your neighbors keep moving away because your community is so dangerous, and you are criticized by family members because you stay in the city . . . that is another story altogether. Compassionate servants are needed. People who will stay the course, suffer with neighbors, and give their lives as an offering to Christ are the kinds of workers that Jesus asked us to pray for. We see the crowds. We know that people are harassed and helpless like sheep without a shepherd. Now, we act. We go. We empty ourselves for those who many will ignore.

This calling to the city to live compassionately is such a critical piece to urban mission. We can pray, have a strong family life, overcome our own brokenness . . . we can understand good mission practice, stay humble . . . these are all images of the Living Christ that we are trying to capture as we journey through this study. But the demands of compassion are great. If our hearts become numb to the pain or jaded towards the very people we have been sent, we will walk away and do something easier.

Our prayer must be that we will truly capture the image of Jesus in compassion. When we see our neighbors, when we see our city, we too should weep. We too can say as Matthew 9:36 says, "When he saw the crowds, he had compassion on them because they were harassed and helpless, like sheep without a shepherd." The compassion that comes from the Spirit can so fill our hearts that we pray for workers and those workers enter into God's mission with Christ-exalting compassion. Jesus chose the most ordinary and even the marginalized of his day. Those he called were not only recipients of his compassion, but he also left the entire mission in their hands, and they changed the world. This is our time.

Chapter 6
REFLECTING HIS IMAGE IN HUMILITY

Zoom-In

When he noticed how the guests picked the places of honor at the table, he told them this parable: "When someone invites you to a wedding feast, do not take the place of honor, for a person more distinguished than you may have been invited. If so, the host who invited both of you will come and say to you, 'Give this person your seat.' Then, humiliated, you will have to take the least important place. But when you are invited, take the lowest place, so that when your host comes, he will say to you, 'Friend, move up to a better place.' Then you will be honored in the presence of all the other guests. For all those who exalt themselves will be humbled, and those who humble themselves will be exalted."

Then Jesus said to his host, "When you give a luncheon or dinner, do not invite your friends, your brothers or sisters, your relatives, or your rich neighbors; if you do, they may invite you back and so you will be repaid. But when you give a banquet, invite the poor, the crippled, the lame, the blind, and you will be blessed. Although they cannot repay you, you will be repaid at the resurrection of the righteous." (Luke 14:7-14)

Servanthood amongst the people of society who are most ignored characterized the life and mission of Jesus. The religious and esteemed in New Testament times had certain cultural norms that needed to be followed. Jesus continually pushes back on such societal tension by welcoming the least prominent, most marginalized, and teaches that a new Kingdom has come. This new Kingdom seeks to establish a new society where a servant-king rules and the last are first (Matt. 20:16). The kind of openness that Jesus models exemplifies itself in acceptance of those who were once threatened and excluded. Now, those very people have found a place of safety.[95]

A Seat at the Table

Several years ago, I got into a sticky situation where there was conflict and pain between me and another leader in my area. I felt devalued and pushed down. I recall a conversation by phone where I asked, "Is there still a seat at the table for me?" Nervousness and anxiety filled my heart. We have all likely asked this question, but Jesus tells a tremendous story to teach humility and what a seat at the table really looks like in the Kingdom of God.

Anyone who knew anything in Jewish society would have known how the social rules were supposed to work in this situation in Luke 14. The seats would be aligned in a "U" with the most prominent folks at the center, and the other elites to the right and to the left.[96] The disabled, poor, and blind that Jesus mentions

---

95. Duane Elmer, *Cross-Cultural Servanthood: Serving the World in Christlike Humility* (Downers Grove, IL: IVP, 2006), 35-36. Elmer explains that humility and servanthood is expressed powerfully in openness, namely Christ dying on the cross. He further shows that such openness allows for those on the margins, or really anyone who has been shielded off, to be accepted and be safe. Safety becomes integral to servanthood.

96. Bock, 399.

would have been assumed to have sin in their lives that have caused their predicament.[97] Jesus instructs through this parable that the overlooked people of society should be the ones to be invited to such a party and that we should never promote ourselves by sitting at the place of honor. We should sit in the lowest position and give priority to the disabled, the blind, and those society considers invisible.

While Jesus outlines some generally good social norms for a myriad of cultures, he really is getting at the heart of the Beatitudes he taught at the Sermon on the Mount. "Blessed are the poor in spirit"—as we display this kind of humility to the world, the forgotten are found, and the humble will be exalted.

The City and the Stigma of the Outcast

Amos Yong, in his tremendous work on theology and disability, has argued well that it is not actually the disabled who have an issue with their disability. It is often the constant reminders they are given from the broader culture that they do not belong or are in some way in need of being rightly put together again.[98] The stigma in modern day urban America has gotten significantly better in terms of there being an equal playing field, a seat at the table if you will, where the disabled and able-bodied can sit side by side. But the cultures of Jesus' day and our own are still not so far removed from one another. On a somewhat frequent basis, I have individuals come up to me, noticing my white cane

---

97. Takatemjen, "Luke" in *South Asia Bible Commentary,* ed. Brian Wintle (Grand Rapids, MI: Zondervan, 2015), Kindle Location 1362-3.

98. Amos Yong, *The Bible, Disability, and the Church: A New Vision of the People of God* (Grand Rapids, MI: William B Eerdmans Publishing Co., 2011), Kindle Location 167-220.

and want me to be healed as they pray. Sometimes I am quoted Scriptures that talk about removing the sin over my life so I can live as a normal person in society. We have all watched as outsiders to our neighborhoods look in horror on the beggar, the prostitute, or the alcoholic. It has been 2,000 years removed and sometimes it seems the stigma is not altogether different.

The humble community that Christ taught for us to be inviting people into is the kind of Kingdom where there is definitely a seat at the table for all. Stigma and labels are shattered. Us and them language is flipped on its head. The poor and rich fellowship together. Humility in Christ's Kingdom, as Jesus taught in this parable, destroys the rules and societal norms of the day. What Jesus is teaching is not so much cosmetics— clearly this is not about assigned seating at all our urban church and ministry functions. This is a posture of Christ that teaches all are welcome, the first will be last, and the humble exalted.

Focusing on the Right Thing

In verses 1-6 of Luke 14, Jesus talks about a man who had dropsy, a condition evidenced by swelling in the body caused by excessive fluid.[99] His presence at such a prominent banquet would have been impossible to ignore. These kinds of gatherings were marked by prestigious guests often joining a discourse of great importance as the elite gathered around.[100] When Jesus teaches who should be invited to such a gathering, he is shifting the focus to where attention should be placed. In delineating that an elite

---

99. Keener, Kindle Location 4854.

100. Keener, Kindle Location 4854.

crowd shouldn't merely invite a prominent person to their party so they can be repaid with gifts, he is calling for a kind of humility that emphasizes the way a Kingdom society should work.[101] Every Jew gathered at this party knows that the righteous will be rewarded at the resurrection. Jesus, however, centers humility and righteousness on a redistribution of resources here and now.[102] The teaching is not new as these ethics were part of Old Testament law. But again, Jesus chooses to teach humility and care for the poor at the most unlikely of times in the most challenging circumstance.

The context of Jesus' ministry up to this point must also be considered as we identify how Christ shifted focus with this parable. The Jews were waiting and waiting for the kingdom only to find themselves preoccupied with other things. Clearly, the Kingdom of God and the arrival of the Messiah were not recognized. As N.T. Wright argues, there were certainly Jews at the time that would be considered followers of Christ, but the vast majority in Palestine as well as Jews scattered elsewhere were simply not present at the banquet Christ was preparing.[103] The party Jesus is inviting people into is unlike any movement the

---

101. Keener, Kindle Location 4854-55. The cultural practice of inviting a prominent, honored guest would have been laying down security for oneself in getting nice gifts that they would bring. Keener argues that in inviting those who cannot repay restructures the entire system and redefines distribution of resources in God's Kingdom.

102. Wayne Gordon and John Perkins, *Making Neighborhoods Whole* (Downers Grove, IL: IVP, 2013), 75-83. The concept of redistribution of resources within the CCDA originates from the life of Christ and the term comes from Gordon and Perkins.

103. N.T. Wright, *Luke for Everyone: The New Testament for Everyone* (Louisville, KY: John Knox Press, 2004), 178-179.

world had ever seen. People radically different from each other socially, economically, ethnically, even religiously are invited to the banquet. The focus is shifted from the elite to the lowly. Wright admonishes that this is the task of Christians today: "What does it mean for our own churches and families today to celebrate God's Kingdom in such a way that the people at the bottom of the pile, at the end of the line would find it to be Good News?"[104] A humble servant-king calls humble servants to focus on a Kingdom that is as subversive today as it was in first-century Palestine.

Humility From Start to Finish

From his first breath to his last, Christ showed the attitude of a servant in every possible way. Elmer explains that it is not that Christ served to show some sort of virtue, but he served because this is the very nature of God himself.[105] Jesus leaves the glory of heaven and is revealed to the world as a baby born to illegitimate parents. Uprooted from his country, his family flees at the decree of Herod. Christ continually associated with the marginalized of society and faced ridicule for it. In a most uncommon display of honor in his last moments on this earth, Jesus washes the feet of his disciples (Matt. 26:13-39). The Son of God did not open his mouth as the accusations came his way when he stood before Pilate. Finally, he humbles himself to the point of a torturous death on a public cross for all the world to scoff at him.

When Christ taught the Parable of the Great Banquet, he was not speaking of a humility of mere noble intentions. He was talking about his own life, his own attitude, and his own death. As

---

104. Wright, 178.

105. Elmer, 21.

we are continually reminded in our attempt to reflect Jesus in the city, the way of Christ is the way of the cross. Servanthood is most expressed in surrender, in denial of rights, yes, even in death.

The beauty of such surrender though is that Jesus is exalted and Christ is remembered. The parable here teaches that those who exalt themselves will be humbled, but those who humble themselves will be exalted. In reflecting Christ's example in Word and deed, we identify with his glory and exalt him. The Kingdom reign comes as we walk the humble road.

Zoom-Out

Patrick Fung, referenced in the previous chapter, recalls a story about the unrecognized leaders of mission that made an impact. He once went into a library in England and was doing some research when he noticed rows and rows of files. Before him were the files of the countless number of missionaries who had taken the gospel to China over the previous hundreds of years. The librarian, who was not a believer, approached him and said, "Each file represents one life. One life given fully to the gospel for the Chinese people." Few names anyone would recognize; few are remembered in the story of Christian missions. Fung went on to say that the task before us in missions is going to call for nameless people and unrecognized leadership who make Christ visible not themselves.[106]

Humility was the defining posture of Christ in the incarnation. He humbled himself, was born of a virgin, and lived a life as a poor peasant in Palestine. The lyrics of the worship song

---

106. Fung, "Live to be Forgotten Interview."

"Humble King" from a decade ago summarizes Christ's humility well: "You are the God of the broken, the friend of the weak. You wash the feet of the weary, embrace the ones in need. I want to be like you Jesus, to have this heart in me. You are the God of the humble. You are the humble king."[107]

The actions, teachings, and very nature of Christ himself were one of humility. Such a quality doesn't often make it into the urban ministry biographies of our day, but it is this very attitude which enables us to reflect Christ's image in our cities.

Chris and Krista Ophus

I met Chris about ten years ago when I joined International Teams, my missions sending organization. The first time I saw him, he sat with a Mexican friend from his neighborhood of Little Village in Chicago where he discussed Catholicism with new missionary candidates during an orientation week. I learned later, after becoming good friends with Chris, that he gave his heart to the Lord in late high school after his girlfriend Krista led him to Christ. They were both runners and met through their cross-country team.

Krista grew up in Bolivia as a missionary kid and upon marrying Chris, they both knew they were called to ministry and began to serve in Mexico. Krista was, of course, fluent in Spanish and Chris studied hard to learn Spanish and became a very effective communicator. He now preaches in both English and Spanish each week at the church he pastors. When they were in Mexico working with university students, they began to notice that large portions of villages were abandoned as people migrated to

---

107. Brenton Brown, "Humble King," (Vineyard UK: 1999).

the US. They connected well with the villagers, but they found that many of them were landing back in the Chicago area of Little Village. After serving for two years in Mexico, Chris and Krista returned to Chicago and began working in Little Village.

The Ophus family is brilliant. Krista earned her undergraduate and graduate degrees in education and teaches bilingually at a school in their neighborhood. Chris too holds a BA and MA in intercultural studies from well-known institutions. To just about everyone on the planet, Little Village is a place to avoid. Crime, drugs, murder—all these things and more happen on a daily basis. My family recently visited the Ophus family in their neighborhood and ten murders had happened not far from their house so far that year. Little Village can be a hostile place. Chris and Krista have chosen to buy a home, put their roots down, and announce the Kingdom there.

After seven years of marriage and expecting they may not be able to have children, Krista finally became pregnant with their oldest son, Jonathan. Neither Krista nor Chris spoke English with their son before his first day of kindergarten. They had committed to raising their son bilingually. Their social experiment in parenting worked; they now have three children, all born naturally, who are bilingual. They converse most of the day in Spanish, and they have chosen to live lives of Christlikeness like few I have ever known. Krista could teach at any school district in the country. Chris could be a historian on Chicago or an immigration lawyer. They chose Little Village.

This is the humility of Christ. Chris and Krista are some of the nameless people in our generation. Chris pastors a new church in the neighborhood and things continue to evolve and develop after so many years invested. In the midst of a community that has become the object of political rhetoric, you will never find the Ophus family losing their cool or saying anything out of turn. Humility has found its home in their hearts.

Manika Biswa

Last year I met Manika, a Bhutanese-Nepali immigrant new to Pittsburgh. She grew up in Bhutan, was exiled and lived in a refugee camp in Nepal for twenty years, and now she is here. Her husband left her for another woman, and she has raised her son into an outstanding young man. Her mom struggles with physical and mental disabilities, and most days of the week she can be found caring for her in their home.

Every time my family goes to visit her, Manika drops everything she is doing. She never talks negatively of any of the losses she has experienced. Let's do the math here. She has lost her land, her village, her citizenship, her husband . . . in Nepali culture she has lost her dignity. Somehow the woman who gets jilted always gets the brunt of the gossip even when it is not her fault. Still, Manika stays humble, broken, and pure before the Lord.

This summer, our ministry in Pittsburgh had a college student from Colorado (remember Molly's poem from the intro) come, and she became good friends with Manika. She taught her how to make Nepali food and encouraged her to use the basic Nepali she had developed. Molly will be returning to Pittsburgh for a long-term commitment in the Nepali community. Because of the display of Manika's brokenness before the Lord, Molly's first choice for housing was in the same complex where Manika lives. She knows she will be taken care of and gain a stronger entrance into the community. Manika's continual example of thinking of others first has so captured Molly's heart. In the first five months, she will be Molly's full-time Nepali language instructor. Blessed are the poor in spirit, for theirs is the kingdom of heaven" (Matt. 5:3).

In All Things, Charity

My wife Charity has had an uncharacteristic way of finding her niche in ministry. She is extremely quiet and often people take her silence or lack of emotion for apathy or disinterest. Nothing could be farther from the truth. She doesn't enjoy being the center of attention, and she will rarely speak up when asked in a medium to large sized group. She needs a lot of time to process and will not blab something out unless she is sure of herself. All those dynamics made it difficult for her in our early years of ministry. She often felt like she was supposed to be saying something, being loud, or organizing some big gathering. She would never and will never march to anyone else's beat but her own.

About ten years ago, however, when we began working with refugees, something changed within her. She found herself meeting really practical needs and helping in ways that she never dreamed. Grocery shopping, tutoring, filling out forms, filing taxes . . . the list could go on. I noticed Charity's entire countenance change as she began engaging in the kind of ministry she was wired to do.

God took the humility that she had shown over many years and was able to exalt her into a place of leadership where she became a very powerful voice and presence in the Bhutanese and Karen communities in Minneapolis-St. Paul. I began to notice more people asking about her and wanting her help before my own. This was a crystal clear demonstration of God taking someone who is humble, putting her into a place of influence, and allowing her to thrive. In the early days when this began to happen, it was so evident that a transformation was taking place. God may indeed oppose the proud, but there is grace, so much grace given to those who are humble.

Chris, Krista, Manika, and Charity would never admit that they are humble servants. That is the paradox of such a life. Jesus never claimed to be humble. His life, ministry, teaching, death, and resurrection simply confirmed an incarnation of humility. The unrecognized, nameless, and unheralded urban workers in our day will undoubtedly bring the Kingdom of power to their neighborhoods. "God opposes the proud but shows favor to the humble" (Prov. 3:34; James 4:6) is a posture to hold firm.

Capture His Image

Over and over again, Jesus models and teaches servanthood expressed in humility. No one will argue that one of the central Kingdom currents is surrender; we lay our lives down and humble ourselves. Christ is made visible. Many of us in cross-cultural work in the city, however, bring a lot of baggage. If we have moved into the city as outsiders, we often bring academic degrees, professional training, and sometimes years of experience from other contexts. We have learned to strategize and fix problems as a chief American value. As we enter the city though, we must lay these things down at the feet of Jesus. They are noble, and no doubt these things will be helpful. But let us not be known primarily for our expertise, problem-solving, or academic exploits. May we, just as Jesus instructed and modeled, be known as servants. The privilege that many of us bring to our neighborhoods must be surrendered on an ongoing basis.

The city is also filled with the Manikas, the Eh Paws, and the Haris. These unnoticed servants show us again and again that the way of the Kingdom is not the way of the world. When we surrender and listen, we can all grow together in what God's humble Kingdom is in this time and place. As we meditate on our neighborhoods and Scripture, let's discuss a few more questions to help put this all into practice.

We all bring baggage to the city, things that slow us down from living a life of humility. What are some of the barriers in your life that cause you to be prideful instead of humble?

Who are some of the humble servants, both insiders and outsiders, in your community? Briefly tell their story.

After studying Luke 14, what specific action do you believe the Holy Spirit is leading you into?

What actions or teachings of Jesus stand out to you when thinking about the topic of humility?

It is true that we live in a self-promotional age. Twitter, Facebook, Snapchat . . . a new social media site pops up every day it seems. The centering focus of all these sites is self-promotion. Obviously, these can be used well in networking and ministry, but they often have the reverse effect. In light of those realities, let's reflect on humility for our generation.

How do you feel about social media after reading this chapter on humility? Is there anything you think you would like to change about your self-promoting habits?

Do you feel like your ministry or church ever crosses the line from creating awareness to pride? Why or why not?

What advice would you give to a young person in his use of communication in order to succeed in a life and ministry of humility?

How can you prop up those leaders in your neighborhood who are unrecognized on social media or on ministry websites? How can you come alongside and encourage them, giving them the affirmation they need?

What is the equivalent of washing the disciples' feet in your context? How can you practically carry this out consistently?

To live to be forgotten in order that Christ be remembered is the cry of this chapter. Humility takes discipline, patience, sacrifice, and a lot of prayer. The humble way of the Kingdom doesn't just happen. Perhaps the Spirit is clearly calling us into a deeper level of Christlike ministry. While some of the sacrifices we are making could certainly be applauded by some, we must remember that we are simply servants. Language learning, living in a rough patch of our neighborhood, earning a wage far less than what we are capable of making—these are all sacrifices that we make to reflect Jesus in the city. These are not exploits to be heralded or medals to be worn. We have given up our rights in order that Christ would be remembered not ourselves. May we all become the kinds of servants like Jesus called and clearly reflect his image of humility in the city. The Kingdom party has come as Jesus announced, and it is so visibly displayed through surrender.

Chapter 7
REFLECTING HIS IMAGE IN FAMILY

Zoom-In

While Jesus was still talking to the crowd, his mother and brothers stood outside, wanting to speak to him. Someone told him, "Your mother and brothers are standing outside, wanting to speak to you." He replied to him, "Who is my mother, and who are my brothers?" Pointing to his disciples, he said, "Here are my mother and my brothers. For whoever does the will of my Father in heaven is my brother and sister and mother." (Matt. 12:46-50)

Near the cross of Jesus stood his mother, his mother's sister, Mary the wife of Clopas, and Mary Magdalene. When Jesus saw his mother there, and the disciple whom he loved standing nearby, he said to her, "Woman, here is your son," and to the disciple, "Here is your mother." From that time on, this disciple took her into his home." (John 19:25-27)

Jesus emphasized the Kingdom of God as taking precedent over the nuclear family (Luke 14:26; Matt. 19:29). The decision of the disciples in choosing to leave their families and follow Christ can sometimes be confusing when trying to sort out family health versus ministry pursuit. On the one hand, Jesus will say things like anyone who is not willing to forsake his family is not worthy of me (Luke 14) while he puts a strong priority on the sacredness of marriage and the lives of children as being representative of life in his Kingdom (Matt. 19:3-6; Luke 18:16). Clearly, Christ does not neglect the importance of marriage and the common bond within family as he talked openly about issues of divorce, lust, and often used love of family as a comparison of God's love (Matt. 19:3-12; Matt. 5:28; Mark 10:2; Luke 15:11-32).

There seems to be a tension throughout the Scriptures and quite notably in Jesus' teaching between allegiance to God's Kingdom and nuclear family. There is no perfect model of Christ-centered, God-exalting family anywhere in the Scriptures so we grapple for meaning. The challenge of imperfect families even amongst Christ's own family is no exception. Westfall writes the following:

Jesus' incarnation demonstrates how God works in and through our family ties. The circumstances of the incarnation blow apart family ties and utopian ideals of how God works through the family. Jesus belonged to a family that would be considered dysfunctional rather than ideal, particularly according to cultural standards. He demonstrates that God breaks through and utilizes our imperfect circumstances to accomplish his purposes. He does not require traditional family to qualify us for his kingdom or mission.[108]

In reflecting Christ in the city and capturing his image of family, we too must redefine what Kingdom allegiance is and how to best care for our family's needs in practical ways. As we zoom-in, we will attempt to capture the heart of Jesus' words and actions

---

108. Cynthia Long Westfall, "Family in the Gospels and Acts," in *Family in the Bible: Exploring Customs, Culture, and Context*, ed. Richard S. Hess and M. Daniel Carroll R. (Grand Rapids, MI: Baker Academic, 2003), 146.

about the family understanding that this is one of the most difficult of all Christ's teachings.

Urbanization and the Family in the New Testament

In reading the Gospels, the words "cities and villages" are interlinked emphasizing the socio-political reality that was taking place in regard to urbanization, economic reciprocity, and trade.[109] Matthew 9:35 and 10:11, Mark 6:56, and Luke 10:1 and 13:22 all group city-village together reemphasizing the urban clusters that had developed throughout Israel.[110] This dynamic is incredibly important to the understanding of family in the New Testament as competing values, culture, religion, and linguistic frustrations would have inevitably been part of the experience of those in the Gospels. Ethnicity was inextricably connected to religion thus confirming one's identity.[111] To neglect these tensions of ethnic and urban change is to miss the weight of Jesus' words and actions—particularly his calling to the Kingdom family throughout his ministry.

Village and family life were previously noted in the chapter on prayer and rest. To dive further into that context is important to understand family life in first-century Israel. The context of the Gospels does resemble a family unit much closer to the lives of our immigrant neighbors than what we see in majority culture in the

---

109. Conn and Ortiz, 119.

110. Conn and Ortiz connect the Scriptural framework here in order to explain that in these particular instances, city, town, and village are used in such a way to signify cluster populations thus giving the areas of Jesus' life and ministry a much more urban reality than originally meets the eye.

111. Conn and Ortiz, 119-20.

West. A family would have been thought of more in the concept of an entire village unit as relatives, and extended family would have lived in close proximity to one another.[112] Several one-room buildings would have been connected to each other and likely had a shared courtyard that faced outward towards the street. Passersby would see most interaction except for what would happen inside the home. Compared to the high view of privacy in American culture, it would have seemed almost nonexistent during the culture of Jesus' day. The expectation for children to contribute to the family business and especially to the farming that needed to be done would have been firmly established. Certainly each village had a strong sense of responsibility for raising one another's children and social roles for men, women, girls, and boys were well defined.

Redefining of Family

In Matthew 12, Jesus describes that anyone who does the will of God is his family. He questions who is really his brothers, sisters, or mother. Jesus makes several similar statements to these throughout his life as he establishes his disciples, the family of God, as taking precedent over nuclear family. In doing this, Jesus is confronting where allegiance truly lies. In establishing true disciples as the family of God, he is putting the emphasis on a family that will both be responsible for taking the gospel to the ends of the earth as well as a family that will continue for all eternity (Acts 1:8; Matt. 28:18-20). Jesus tells his listeners that those seeking after the Kingdom of God will leave family behind,

---

112. Carolyn Osiek, "Jesus and Cultural Values: Family Life as an Example," (paper presented at the Images of Jesus Seminar, Research Institute for Theology and Religion, University of South Africa, September 3-4, 1997).

sell all that they have, and that familial relationship should even seem like hate compared to the devotion we have to Christ (Matt. 19:21; Luke 14:26). This teaching is difficult to hear even in independent Western cultures where there are not great expectations put on sons and daughters to be the sole providers of aging parents or be obligated to the family business. How much more so this teaching would have been in the face of well-defined roles for the family. Christ's purpose in doing so was to establish one allegiance to one family, the Kingdom of God.

Another reality in the life of Christ is that Jesus was not treated well by the villagers and the townspeople. Osiek argues that Jesus was considered an illegitimate son by his own family. She espouses that with the exception of James and Mary, that Jesus would have been an embarrassment for his home village, explaining Christ's return to Nazareth to be devastating.[113] Jesus takes on a surrogate family with the disciples as they ate, drank, slept, and ministered together. While Christ redefines family as "anyone who does the will of God," there were certainly very natural, practical reasons for Christ seeming disengaged with his family at times.

One of the most challenging pieces for those within urban neighborhoods or those who choose to relocate will be how to stay faithful to God's call amid close family ties. For the urban worker from the neighborhood, family will often wonder why they don't leave the hood, make some money, and live the good life. For cross-cultural workers who decide to relocate from other cities, neighborhoods, or countries, mom and dad will likely be the

---

113. Osiek, "Jesus and Cultural Values: Family Life as an Example."

strongest barrier.[114] While there are many supportive parents, choosing a life of sacrifice far away from family, sometimes in very dangerous areas, is not typically the way the average family thinks about the welfare of their children. Jesus' call to abandon everything for him and having one allegiance has not changed. The sacrifices disciples must make to follow Jesus are costly in every generation.

Whoever Does the Will of God

Matthew 12:46-50 paints a picture of Jesus saying the most unusual of things about the family. When he says that whoever does the will of God is his family, he is downplaying the role of his mother and brothers who were waiting for him in this instance. Keener notes that given the strong cultural bonds of kinship and hierarchy, Christ's merely giving this image as an example would have been incredibly offensive.[115] Jesus does not simply group members of the disciples as the true family of God, but he lays out a specific behavior and character. Doing the will of God, as consistent in Matthew's writing, is to obey the commands of God by following Jesus.[116] In rooting true family in obedience to God by following Him, Christ establishes himself as the supreme Lord and the cornerstone of the family. This clarion call also displays the nature of the Church, the true family of God. Such loyalty and kinship displays to the world that God's spiritual

---

114. Kim Ransleben, "The Biggest Barrier for Students Going to the Mission Field," *Desiring God,* January 15, 2015, accessed February 22, 2017, http://www.desiringgod.org/articles/the-biggest-barrier-to-students-going-to-the-mission-field.

115. Keener, Kindle Location 1208.

116. Blomberg, 208.

family follows Jesus and his actions are reflected in all we say and do.

Such verses must be held with the utmost care as we live in the world in deep relationship with our nuclear family. We also are part of a greater Kingdom that includes all who follow the commands of Christ. Following Jesus does not neglect husbands, wives, or children. Rather, it serves them in Calvary love, continually laying our lives down for each other. As precious of a picture as that is, however, Christ's image of the family is more robust, more inclusive, and more self-sacrificing than we often know. Truly, the family that Jesus defined was composed of whoever does the will of God.

Providing and Caring for the Nuclear Family

Jesus calls us to a pathway that neither the audience of the first century nor readers today can fully comprehend. Perhaps the most visible and inclusive picture of Jesus on the topic of family is his hanging on a cross and giving his mother away to his disciple John. Historians place Mary at around forty years of age and likely a widow at this time. Jesus orally giving his mother away to John in the presence of witnesses would have made it legally binding.[117] As the eldest son, it would be the responsibility of Jesus to care for his family. Jesus' younger brothers would be around to share in the responsibility of caring for their mother, but Jesus places a disciple he loved very much into the realm of his immediate family. This act combines the previous teaching Jesus had given on how the family of God, those who are following the commands of his Father, are the true spiritual family. Now, as Jesus goes to

---

117. Keener, Kindle Location 5730.

the cross, he blends the spiritual and physical family in a beautiful display of love and responsibility.

This final act before Christ dies displays his deep love for his mother. He knows the cultural ramifications of what his departure means. He does not merely give his mother to his younger brothers, but confirms the disciples to be the true family that will look after his own mother even until her death. For Jesus, it seems that followers of Jesus take on the true role of Christlike community. In inviting John to care for his mother, Mary is now included into the family of disciples and will undoubtedly have influence in the days and years to come.[118]

This aspect of spiritual family being blended with physical family has been an area in missions that brings a lot of controversy. Our urban settings, however, especially when we are rooted in our own host cultures, iron out some of these difficulties. When we serve in urban mission, we are often stepping into situations where there are widows, homeless populations, orphans, or others in dire circumstances where they are in need of a true physical family. It seems irresponsible to build an entire theology of family and care for the orphaned on this exchange at the cross, but at the least we have to consider the kind of family we are becoming. If Christ made no distinction between spiritual and physical family, should we make one? This brings up all sorts of issues in regard to family health, boundaries, sustainability, dependence, and so forth. To reflect Jesus at the cross and blur the lines of immediate and spiritual family though seems to be a cost that we must be willing to count. To completely ignore our brothers and sisters who have no family is not a solution. Perhaps

---

118. Pratap C. Gine and Jacob Cherian, "John" in *South Asia Bible Commentary*, ed. Brian Wintle (Grand Rapids, MI: Zondervan, 2015), 1142.

there are other alternatives than to house everyone in the city in our spare bedroom. Following Jesus in family requires that this be more than a conversation.

Love of family, spiritual and physical, was communicated in the actions and teachings of Christ. Jesus spoke directly about divorce. He confronted adultery and lust head-on. He valued children as precious gifts to his Kingdom. His mother was with him until the very end, and he made provision for her. Every effort should be made to love our immediate family well in the midst of urban ministry. As we do this, there is also a clear calling to redefine the family as Jesus did as being whoever does the will of God. Lifestyle, ministry practice, and theological reflection that includes a strong understanding of family are essential if we are to reflect Christ well in the city.

Zoom-Out

You can choose your friends, but you can't choose your family. Many of us have definitely said these words with a smirk on our face, and certainly there is some truth there that we may not want to admit.[119] Family life, as beautiful as it can be, is difficult. From the first generation of recorded history in Genesis all the way through the New Testament, we find people struggling to get along and reflect the image of God to the world. Jesus, as our Immanuel God always does, shows us the way through the

---

119. Phillip Harold, "You Can't Choose Your Friends," *Patheos Evangelical,* October 11, 2013, accessed February 23, 2017, http://www.patheos.com/blogs/fareforward/2013/10/you-cant-choose-your-friends/. Though the adage of choosing friends and being unable to choose your family gets a chuckle, Harold discusses the reality that we choose neither and are pushed to enter mutually beneficial sacrifices in relationship.

forest. Family is redefined, and we find ourselves longing to participate in such a beautiful Kingdom invitation.

Family Life in Urban Centers

Though Christ's family invitation is desirable and compelling, our cities today can seem quite distant from the imagined future Christ has for us. Most of the world lives in close proximity to their loved ones with many cultures sharing the same house with multiple generations.[120] It is a normal expectation for Asians, Africans, and Latinos to move in with the bride or groom's extended family upon their consummation in marriage. Many of these cultures have now found their way to urban America and that is changing the landscape day by day. Families bring a long history of such familial culture to our cities often amid family discord, crime, drugs, and sexual promiscuity that were not as out in the open in their homelands. Discord has been there all along as it exists in every society. In urban America, however, the band-aid is ripped off and family problems can become very visible as people live in close quarters.

Recently, I was chatting with Hari, my Nepali neighbor, and I made the observation that many of the teenagers are much more sexually active than they were back in Nepal. Drinking, smoking, and having friends wait outside an apartment or house while teens are inside doing their business is not uncommon. I asked my neighbor about this and said, "Nepali values aren't

---

120. Marcia Carteret, "Culture and Family Dynamics," *Dimensions of Culture,* accessed February 23, 2017, http://www.dimensionsofculture.com/2010/11/culture-and-family-dynamics/. Carteret outlines the multi-generational aspects of Asian, African, and Hispanic cultures but points to the shifts that take place within families once acculturated to the US.

altogether different simply because they are in a new country, are they? Why are parents allowing this to happen?"

My friend paused. "The answer is simple, but it is complicated too. You know that the elders in the community were the most respected members of society back in Nepal. Everyone listened to them. Now, they have come to a country where they cannot function well in English. They don't know what is happening too much with their kids' schoolwork. They have their teenage sons and daughters sorting out all the mail and helping organize bills. In my opinion, John, I think the elders are frightened. They are scared if they speak up and push back too hard on their children that their kids will simply leave them. They'll run away and get married and leave the parents alone."

"So Hari, what you are telling me," I responded, "is that the entire authority of cultural norms is being flipped upside down? Elders are no longer being respected and the young people who can speak English are now leading the way?"

"Well, I had never really thought of it that way *dhaju* (older brother), but I guess that is what is happening," Hari said.

This kind of situation is common in the lives of immigrants throughout our cities. There have been some tremendously huge role shifts, and the elders often get the short end of the stick.[121] My pastor recently discussed the generational gaps between parents and kids with me. I had been noticing that Nepali children, even though they had only been in the US for less than five to seven

---

121. Hispanic, Somali, Burmese, Nepali, and Hmong elders have lamented to me and co-workers that in coming to the US, they did it for their children. While their grandchildren and kids have found a rhythm, many still struggle to find an identity having much of their authority pulled from their grasp upon arrival in a country where they do not understand language, culture, and systematic processes.

years, were already poor Nepali communicators. I observed that they did not know basic Nepali vocabulary and that they were struggling to understand their own parents. My pastor told me that his eldest daughter who is only in third grade can likely only understand 30-40% of what he says.

Colleagues and friends have shared these dynamics with me in cities across the country in Asian, Hispanic, and African immigrant communities. The very fabric of authority and power gets shifted and family life can be stressful. Chris from Little Village talked about raising their children bilingually as well as others in his Mexican neighborhood who try to do the same. He mentioned that the first kid holds onto language and culture pretty easily but as the first child starts school and other kids come along, the kids begin to speak English together thus losing their parents' mother tongue. Chris chuckled when he said, "If English can thrive in Little Village and Spanish has a hard time surviving, I have a hard time believing that Spanish is going to take over America anytime soon." Language, culture, and parental authority in urban America are some of the more critical issues in urban family life today.

The Adhikari Family

I will never forget the first time I met Sila. She was a cool, confident eighteen year old walking outside a mostly Burmese and Nepali occupied apartment complex. She carried herself in such a way that I thought she had been in the country for a few years. My wife and I hit it off with her from the very beginning, and we began spending at least two evenings a week with her and her family in their apartment. At first, our time was spent trying to meet practical needs since they had just arrived in the US as refugees.

Shopping for groceries, filling out forms, helping with homework, making trips to government offices—we did all that. But as hours turned into weeks, weeks into months, and months into years, the Adhikaris taught us what it is to be a good family. Though they are Hindu, they lay their lives down for each other and have shown us over nearly a decade now what it is to love your family well.

The Adhikaris had six people living in their two-bedroom apartment in Minnesota. Grandma was extremely ill from the moment she arrived in the country. She had a huge growth on her neck and spent a lot of time in bed. We watched over a couple years' time how much her granddaughters cared for her. We were together all the time. Surely when you hang out with friends and family this much, you are bound to see one of the granddaughters have an off day. Grandma would call from the back room "*Nani* (baby/young girl), come!" No matter which granddaughter it was, they would quickly run to the back room to give her food, sit with her, or simply do the request she asked. The granddaughters were seventeen, eighteen, and twenty-three at the time. I had never before witnessed such love, care, and respect for elders.

Pashupati, the father of the home, continually showed humility and love for his daughters as he encouraged them to get an education and provided hospitality for anyone who entered their apartment. The Adhikaris became a real problem for me and my faith because I started to see that I had never met any family who loved like this. They gave and gave, sacrificing far more than I had ever witnessed. They were never too busy for each other. It was a beautiful display for my own family of what Christ's love looks like. In the end, I had to reconcile that though they are not believers, somehow God had allowed a glimpse of his Kingdom to be displayed through them. Because of the radiant love and care they showed, my family has been forever changed. The Adhikaris now live in Pittsburgh up the road from us, and we see them often.

Colliding Values

The hospitality and visitation that happens within the Asian and Hispanic communities represented in this book are beautiful things to behold. The family lifestyles are quickly changing as America is an independent society, and it becomes increasingly more difficult to keep some of the values that were brought to our cities.[122] About a year ago, I had a neighbor tell me that he could no longer have any kind of control over his children because he couldn't beat his kids any more. He viewed our laws in America on child abuse as barriers for him and his family to establish discipline. His solution was simply to just let his kids watch TV, keep them occupied, and hopefully not get in trouble with the law when he did occasionally lose it and revert to the disciplinarian measures of his host culture. I could sense the tension in his voice as he explained the situation.

The church where we serve is a first-generation Nepali congregation, and we have come alongside to develop youth and children's programs. Only within the last few years has this Hindu background congregation come to Christ. Student ministries are new, and there is a huge learning curve. About two months ago, my wife, who has an elementary education background, made the observation that sibling roles have shifted. In Bhutan and Nepal, teens were the ones who looked   after and cared for the younger children while their mothers worked in the field. In villages

---

122. Kristin McCarthy, "Adaptation of Immigrant Children to the United States: A Review of the Literature" (Working Paper #98-03, Center for Research on Child Well-Being, March 1998), accessed February 23, 2017, http://crcw.princeton.edu/workingpapers/WP98-03-McCarthy.pdf

throughout the country you can see young teens caring for groups of five or six siblings or relatives with no parents ever in sight. It seems that parents are often entrusting that same kind of responsibility here in the States, but it isn't working so well. Students have gained more independence; they have stronger roles as leaders in guiding their elders through an English system in a new country, and the level of respect has significantly dropped. At this point, parents are not involved at all in the youth and children's ministries of our church as there is an expectation for the teens to get the job done. What would be culturally normal in Nepal is not so normal in urban America. We are continually walking between these two cultures, old school Nepal and new school America, to try to ensure that parents are heavily involved in the lives of their children. The gaps continue to widen, respect continues to be lost, and American and Nepali cultural values collide. Welcome to the city they say.

As family authority roles shift, language struggle creates extreme gaps in relationship, and survival seems to rule the day. Thriving as Christ-centered families can seem far removed from reality. We do see occasional glory stories such as the Adhikaris, but more often than not we see three steps forward and two steps back, or at least it feels that way, when it comes to family. Immediate relatives provide a daily litmus test on the authenticity of the gospel because there is no place to hide. You can choose your friends, but you cannot choose your family.

Jesus though, yet again, sets an example for us. When he came to the earth, born of a virgin and despised by many, he shows us on several occasions what it means to follow him in familial relationships. He redefines family in the Kingdom of God through his teaching. He cares for his family well by giving John to look after his mother at the cross. In the most unlikely beckoning, Jesus actually does choose his family, and he shows ever so clearly what is meant by life in the family of God. As we attempt to capture his image in discussion, let us take all these challenges into the presence of God and allow him to breathe new life into our families.

Capture His Image

Let's say it again together. We are not the Messiah. I am not Jesus. You are not Jesus. Following him is difficult. The demands of discipleship and reflecting him in prayer, in suffering, in compassion . . . these are no pursuits for the faint of heart. Reflecting Jesus in family is no different. We are living in cities and cultures where the importance of family has been eroded. Divorce rates are extremely high, and it is completely normal for children to grow up without a father. No one says it out loud, but as we sit in weddings, we all likely have some cynicism in the back of our minds. "I wonder how long they'll make it," we think. On the flip side, we have a Christian worldview that sometimes elevates the nuclear family to the realm of God. Everything centers around this nuclear family, and we do everything possible to ensure happiness, security, and safety.[123] Neither of these extremes is what Jesus taught. Though we are not the Messiah, we still can, with the grace that he offers, reflect Jesus to the world in our families.

A good starting point in following Jesus in his concept of family is to begin to fall in love with Jesus and his mission afresh. Something in the disciples and first-century believers caused them to sell everything, leave family, and become disciples of Christ. Men and women loved their families as most of us do. But there was something that captured their hearts in a way that is inexplicable. That inexplicable transformation caused the disciples to go against the grain of cultural norms and place a priority on the Kingdom of God. The surrogate family of the Church became the

---

123. John Huckins, "Worshipping the Idol of Safety," *Sojourners*, March 23, 2016, accessed February 24, 2017, https://sojo.net/articles/worshiping-idol-safety.

family of God. Somehow, we have to be so captured by the life and love of Jesus that we don't allow cynicism of the family or safety for that matter to dominate. We must place our allegiance in Christ and begin to live as a family of Christ together. In the end, the disciples rebounded from their denial of Jesus at the cross and ended up giving their lives for the gospel. As we think of that commitment, let us discuss together the challenges and action before us in reflecting Jesus in family.

Have you been part of a Christian community that you feel is on the right track in being a true family of God? How so?

What qualities and characteristics make up a good family as Jesus defined it?

What are some of the practices of Jesus that stand out to you in how he loved and served his surrogate family?

Anyone who does the will of God—who is that in your life right now? How can you display a better family lifestyle with them?

What do you sense the Holy Spirit saying to you in reading this chapter? How do you need to obey?

Jesus did not neglect his nuclear family. As we studied, Jesus asked one of his disciples to take care of his mother as his own. He had life-giving compassion on the crowds and many who brought family members to him in the midst of their distress. Our families are not perfect. Sometimes our families do not understand the kind of life we have chosen in following Jesus to the city. For those of us raising our families in such contexts, we face daily challenges that sometimes cause us to question the decision to remain there. This next set of questions require a certain amount of vulnerability. Answer the questions honestly and stay engaged with those as you discuss.

Do your relatives, parents, and friends approve of your doing urban missions? How have you dealt with this and have you had healthy conversations with them about it?

How are you caring for your immediate family? Are you taking care of them physically, emotionally, sexually (for spouses), and economically? Elaborate.

How are you doing with including neighbors, friends, and Christians around you as part of your family?

Turn to your family members (give them a call if they are not present) and ask them some of these same questions. Ask them to answer you honestly about taking care of them in the midst of the city.

What healthy boundaries have you established or do you need to establish to ensure that your immediate family is well cared for?

Jesus lived in a time when there were political, social, and economic realities pressing hard on the family. Urbanization, language struggle, and the roles of family members were shifting. As we saw through stories from our contemporary setting, these things are happening in our cities today. Respond briefly to the contextual issues you are facing in light of God's plan for his family.

How do you see the roles of the family being confused in your context? What do we learn from Christ's words from this chapter that speak into those situations?

How does difficulty with English or immigrants forgetting their parents' mother tongue influence your ministry? What is the best way that you can care for families as they walk down this difficult road?

What cultural shifts are you witnessing in the lives of families involved in your ministry? What practical steps can you bring as you walk alongside them in these cultural adjustments?

For the widow, the orphan, and others who have no physical family and nowhere to go, what does a theology of the family say to that situation? What solutions can be brought for those in these situations as it relates to the family of God?

Sorting through family challenges in the context of immigration in our cities requires missiological alertness, spiritual tenacity, and the patience of the Holy Spirit. The tensions will not go away just because teens and children watch more American TV or expose themselves more to American Christianity. In fact, those things could even magnify the contextual issues in our families. Jesus never lost sight of his mission from birth to the cross. Everything in the incarnation would eventually lead to the transformation of the world. Jesus' redefinition of the family calls us to a higher road which includes the "us and them" language of the world being shattered. There is a new community being created in God's Kingdom, and it is not solely concerned for the well-being of our immediate family. It is concerned for that, but it is far more inclusive and inviting. To capture the image of Christ in family is to lay down your life for your husband, your wife, and your children . . . to lay down our lives for our neighbors, our friends, even our enemies. This Kingdom family that is characterized by "anyone who does the will of God" is the most beautiful invitation we've ever been given and our response must be one of gratitude, sacrifice, and welcome.

Chapter 8
REFLECTING HIS IMAGE IN JUSTICE

Zoom-In

When it was almost time for the Jewish Passover, Jesus went up to Jerusalem. In the temple courts he found people selling cattle, sheep and doves, and others sitting at tables exchanging money. So he made a whip out of cords, and drove all from the temple courts, both sheep and cattle; he scattered the coins of the money changers and overturned their tables. To those who sold doves he said, "Get these out of here! Stop turning my Father's house into a market!" His disciples remembered that it is written: "Zeal for your house will consume me."

The Jews then responded to him, "What sign can you show us to prove your authority to do all this?"

Jesus answered them, "Destroy this temple, and I will raise it again in three days."

They replied, "It has taken forty-six years to build this temple, and you are going to raise it in three days?" But the temple he had spoken of was his body. After he was raised from the dead, his disciples recalled what he had said. Then they believed the scripture and the words that Jesus had spoken. (John 2:13-22)

Jesus and the Temple

The temple in first-century Judaism was the center of all things religious and political having great economic influence throughout Israel. Jesus approaches the temple during the time of Passover wherein the population of Jerusalem may have swelled from 25,000 to 180,000 during the religious holiday.[124] This was no ordinary day wherein Jesus chose to demonstrate his frustration for a broken system. The temple was something to behold resembling more of a plaza than a church building, and the crowd would have been electric during Passover. Jesus enters the epicenter of such institutional power and goes to work.

On any given day, thirty priests could be found working in the temple. During the Passover though, much more action would have been taking place with peddlers selling animals to be sacrificed, Gentile portions of the temple being opened up for commerce, and the overall sense of a house of prayer for all nations (Jer. 7:11; Isa. 56:7) was not realized.[125] The commercialization of worship is certainly addressed along with the implementation of the sacrificial system. Most scholars agree that the crux is not on the sacrificial system or even the obtaining of animals for such sacrifices, but Jesus is angry because the entire system of worship was being subjugated by an institution that was supposed to manifest the glory and presence of God. Religion and sacrifice were completely out of sync with the very Kingdom Jesus

---

124. Donald Kraybill, *The Upside-Down Kingdom*, rev. ed. (Harrisburgh, VA: Herald Press, 2011), 59.

125. Kraybill, 58-59.

had come to inaugurate.[126] The finger must be pointed at religious leaders who knew full well what was happening in such a system. Jesus is angry at the entire project; he takes time to make a whip likely contemplating what he is about to do (John 2:15). He was deliberate in his prophetic pronouncement and declares that judgment is upon them.

The scene and demonstration would have been considered nothing less of blasphemy to those involved in such a political system.[127] The temple was paralleled by none other than Solomon's temple and the five-acre religious metropolis was the pride and joy of religious politicians. Jesus flips the injustice on its head and says it is all wrong. He calls to return to prayer and to welcome Gentiles. He announces the temple as "my house" (Matt. 21:13) indicating his Messiahship and that he will die and be raised again from the dead in three days. Just as in Jesus' day, we have religious and political systems that oppress the poor, exclude those from worship, and seek after political gain. Even to the evangelical church, to mission agencies, and to the business of urban mission, there must be a prophetic voice that cries out, "This is not what Jesus came to do; this is not what the resurrection established. On my watch and in the name of Jesus, stop!"

The prophetic voice in incarnational mission requires Spirit sensitivity and supernatural wisdom from on high. We are not the Messiah, and we must know when it is time to speak and when to listen. Despite those tensions, however, injustice abounds in many of our systems. There is freedom for the captor. Dealing

---

126. Jonathan Parnell, "Jesus Turns the Tables," *Desiring God,* March 30, 2015, accessed February 28, 2017, http://www.desiringgod.org/articles/jesus-turns-the-tables.

127. Keener, Kindle Location 4826.

with captors in the right way is the complexity in all this. Do we approach captors with compassion? Do we approach them with prophetic flare? What do we do when such powers refuse to release the captives in our city? We will continue that conversation in our final section in capturing his image. Let us now look towards injustice upon the captives in our urban contexts.

On one occasion an expert in the law stood up to test Jesus. "Teacher," he asked, "what must I do to inherit eternal life?"

"What is written in the Law?" he replied. "How do you read it?"

He answered, "'Love the Lord your God with all your heart and with all your soul and with all your strength and with all your mind'; and, 'Love your neighbor as yourself.'"

"You have answered correctly," Jesus replied. "Do this and you will live."

But he wanted to justify himself, so he asked Jesus, "And who is my neighbor?"

In reply Jesus said: "A man was going down from Jerusalem to Jericho, when he was attacked by robbers. They stripped him of his clothes, beat him and went away, leaving him half dead. A priest happened to be going down the same road, and when he saw the man, he passed by on the other side. So too, a Levite, when he came to the place and saw him, passed by on the other side. But a Samaritan, as he traveled, came where the man was; and when he saw him, he took pity on him. He went to him and bandaged his wounds, pouring on oil and wine. Then he put the man on his own donkey, brought him to an inn and took care of him. The next day he took out two denarii and gave them to the innkeeper. 'Look after him,' he said, 'and when I return, I will reimburse you for any extra expense you may have.'

"Which of these three do you think was a neighbor to the man who fell into the hands of robbers?"

The expert in the law replied, "The one who had mercy on him."

Jesus told him, "Go and do likewise." (Luke 10:25-37)

Declaring Justice by Showing Mercy to Those who are Held Captive

Jesus attacks injustice from several angles when he tells the Parable of the Good Samaritan, giving insight to the issues of power, race, compassion, and apathy. Christ uses the questions of the spiritual elite to take head-on what mission is all about. "What is eternal life" and "who is my neighbor" are the two questions that we need to sort out in responding to the issues of justice in our time.

Justice, often translated as righteousness, is not solely an earthly issue.[128] Some of the debates over social justice, liberation theology, and the physical versus the spiritual in ministry neglect justice as a discipleship, Jesus-transformation kind of issue. In order to really grasp the weight of the biblical text in regard to justice, we must understand its inseparable tie to salvation. Listen to Lim as he comments on the Isaiah 56:1 (NRSV) passage:

Thus says the LORD: Maintain justice, and do what is right, for soon my salvation will come, and my deliverance be revealed. In order for God's salvation to be fully realized, injustice

---

128. Timothy Keller, *Generous Justice: How God's Grace Makes Us Just* (New York, NY: Penguin Books, 2010), Kindle Location 75.

must be dealt with—first and foremost its presence among the people of God. Why? Because the goal of Yahweh's salvation is not the eternal security of one's soul or merely living a better existence on earth, but rather to be brought to dwell on God's holy mountain.[129]

Prophets like Isaiah, Amos, and Micah called for a just society that was locked together with the salvation of God. The establishment of God's reign is evidenced through justice being shown throughout every level of the community. Luke 10 and the Parable of the Good Samaritan further the message of the prophets.

The answer to the questions of eternal life and what classifies someone as our neighbor are answered clearly in the parable. In knowing nothing about the identity of the man who was robbed, we cannot pigeonhole Jesus to give us a narrow definition in regard to whom we should show justice and mercy. Lavine asserts that in Jesus not classifying the man who was robbed, he calls his listeners and readers to define a neighbor as "some man" or "anyone" for that matter. Anyone within his audience would have known this seventeen-mile walk all too well, and our neighbor becomes anyone who may be walking along the road.[130] In answering the question of eternal life in the name of

---

129. Bo Lim, "A Return to Justice and Righteousness," Seattle Pacific University Lectio, accessed March 1, 2017, http://blog.spu.edu/lectio/a-return-to-justice-and-righteousness/.

130. Amy Lavine, *Short Stories By Jesus: The Enigmatic Parables of a Controversial Rabbi* (New York: Harper Collins, 2014), 87-88. Lavine challenges the reader to pay careful attention to the stranger being anonymous making implications that all people should be regarded as a neighbor.

love and mercy, a neighbor is redefined, and we stand before a just God who woos us to be merciful. Eternal life is evidenced in the life of the person who doesn't try to flee from the question by implying who his neighbor is not. Perhaps that is a polite way to interpret the teacher of the law's question here.[131] Jesus responds by initiating a just Kingdom that is characterized through the most unlikely and reviled of people. Though despised and lowly to many hearers of the day, this Kingdom reign is shown through viewing anyone in need as our neighbor and true justice being established through action.

A Neighbor's Heart

In reflecting Jesus in justice, it is imperative that we not miss the root issue. The entire parable is motivated by an answer to the questions of eternal life, love, and neighborliness. To Jesus' listeners, a Samaritan would have been the most unexpected of all people to show forth the justice of God in this situation. Jesus points to the Samaritan going above and beyond what many would expect from a good neighbor. He takes care of the stranger's wounds, takes the stranger to an inn to be cared for, and gives him enough money for the next two weeks as he recovers (Luke 10:34-35). The justice of God for the one being held captive is one of mercy and seeing as well as responding to those in need.

The heart of the Samaritan takes the love of God and expresses itself in the midst of difficulty and danger. Bock compares the seventeen-mile stretch from Jericho to Jerusalem to none other than an inner city.[132] Robbers, muggings, and the like

---

131. Lavine, 80.

132. Bock, 300.

were commonplace. To anyone walking this difficult stretch, the tendency could have been to simply get through the area safely and continue on the journey. Jesus' teaching though is that being a good neighbor is stepping into the pain, danger, and difficulty and showing mercy.

Freedom for Captives and Captors

Jesus shows his justice to both captive and captor. He confronts macro issues that can only be dealt with by a re-creation of society. He calls for his followers to see one person and love them without limit. As Jesus seems to always be able to do in his life and teaching, he shoots in both directions compelling all involved to participate. This is yet again the Kingdom invitation for the city.

We have no shortage of injustice before us. Just as was happening in Jesus' day, racism abounds. Injustice, broken systems, and the marginalization of entire blocs of society knock on our doors. The path to Jericho is dangerous, but there are many who have fallen into the hands of robbers in our communities. Institutions and systems have often caused the misery. Let us shift gears as we contemplate contextual issues of justice in our neighborhoods.

Zoom-Out

My son is named Amos. We like cookies (grandpa cannot stop buying us boxes of Famous Amos) and the name wasn't super popular, but contrary to popular opinion, this is not the real reason why we gave him this name. The prophet Amos was deeply concerned about justice. A theme verse for us and many in the urban context is Amos 5:24, "But let justice roll on like a river, righteousness like a never-failing stream!" Having our own flesh and blood that has a name associated with this kind of justice and righteousness, we feel is one of our better decisions. The prophet Micah instructs us to both seek justice and love mercy simultaneously (Mic. 6:8). Tim Keller expands on the marriage of mercy and justice being both an attitude as well as action which brings healing to all involved.[133] Our cities find themselves amid people and situations desperate for the justice of God, revealed in Jesus, to come to its gates. Attitudes and postures of love blended with the active righteousness of God is the call of justice in Christlike mission.

Unjust Systems in Leadership Development in Urban Mission

In capturing the image of Christ in compassion in chapter 5, we looked at Matthew 9:36 which is a cry for those who are harassed and helpless to have a shepherd. Leadership in the urban context is a critical issue and oftentimes parachurch and mission organizations establish a presence in city neighborhoods by employing full-time workers through the traditional support raising model. Erick Robinson has researched and presented on this topic and calls for action on the empowerment of ethnic minorities in missional leadership. He roots his research in the gap between whites and ethnic minorities, which according to a 2011 Pew report, placed whites at having twenty times more

---

133. Keller, *Generous Justice*, Kindle Location 4.

wealth on the average than many Latino and African-Americans.[134] Listen to Robinson's explanation of the injustice:

The personal support raising model is built on the idea that each missionary has a social network they can leverage to pray for them, give financially to fund the ministry, and provide them referrals to expand the network . . . The organization provides no other mechanism to provide financially for the staff member. If the potential missionary is unable to raise their full financial support, they cannot join staff with the organization. Many mission leaders view this as an equitable, just system and have been hesitant to making changes. Often their rationale sounds something like, "Everyone needs to start from the same place, to raise their own support. It wouldn't be fair to give some an advantage." But there's a major flaw in that logic: we don't all start from the same place.[135]

The ramifications of ignoring this disparity has the potential to erode the very compassionate mission that many of our urban ministries are attempting to bring to the city. In saying things like we are for the marginalized, we love the broken, and we have come to declare justice, yet when we look around at our leadership and it does not reflect who is represented in our communities, are we really seeking justice? As Robinson notes, the time has come for us to deal head-on with such disparity and find solutions. I would argue that in ignoring this issue in our

---

134. Erick Robinson, "How Support-Raising Keeps Parachurch Ministries White," *Minister Different: Pursuing Justice in Support-Raising*, accessed March 21, 2017, http://ministerdifferent.com/support-raising-white/. Robinson quotes Pew Research from 2011 citing that middle-class whites often have twenty times the amount of access to funding because the wealth is twenty times greater in white communities versus ethnic communities. His argument here is that we clearly do not all start from the same place economically and that disparity should be addressed.

135. Ibid.

contemporary contexts, we nullify many of the other ministries of justice to the orphan, the widow, the refugee, and the disabled. Urban mission has never been and never will be nice and tidy. It requires difficult decisions and sacrifices. Without question, people will be offended along the way.

Slumlords Exist

Several apartment complexes on the north side of St. Paul house the Karen people of Burma as well as many Bhutanese-Nepali refugees. Few of the complexes have on-site landlords, and the living conditions are often atrocious. In our years in the Twin Cities, I walked past a puddle of vomit in the hallway in one complex that had not been cleaned up in days. Mice were a nightly occurrence in most people's homes, and the refugee occupants just learned to tolerate the annoyance as it seemed pretty well compared to their previous refugee camps. Bedbugs were commonplace. Repairs were neglected even after residents filed reports.

I once was staying with a youth pastor and a couple guys from his youth group at a Karen family's apartment. I knew the apartment was rough, but I'd never stayed the night. There were a handful of young people helping our church for the weekend, and this was a good way for them to get to know the culture and lifestyle of those in our community. Once we turned the lights off and went to bed, more roaches than we'd ever seen emerged. Along the edges of the entire wall of the room were hundreds of critters. When I got up to use the bathroom at night, I felt a couple of roaches under my fingertips as I flipped the light on, and I could hear more scurrying towards the drain as I entered the doorway. These were just the normal living conditions of our friends.

After this experience combined with many others, I got in touch with the city and our ministry had a direct line to inspectors who would quickly go after the slumlords. It wasn't the most transformational thing that has ever been done, but it was a start. Few newly arrived refugees and immigrants will say much for fear of getting kicked out of their apartments. Because they have never been in the home of an American or even been to a majority American occupied apartment complex, they lack the frame of reference for what should qualify as a good standard of living.[136] Such living conditions are unjust in our society and a voice to speak is required.

The Return of Eh Paw

Remember Eh Paw from a few chapters ago? As a teenager, he came to the US by himself; now he is a key leader in the Karen refugee community in St. Paul. Eh Paw came to my house one night with a friend of ours who also attended our church. Our friend Lisa was a PhD student and had worked in social work amongst refugees for years. She is a mover and a shaker and gets things done in the inner city. I have rarely seen such commitment and love as she pours her life out for the Somali, Karen, and Nepali communities in the Twin Cities. When Lisa and Eh Paw arrived, we had planned to order some food. My wife would join us when she got off work. Eh Paw got a call on the way, and he found out that a Karen lady brand new to the country was lost and roaming around St. Paul somewhere.

---

136. Andrea Castillo, Barbara Anderson, and Bonhia Lee, "Apartments Crawling with Mice, Roaches, but Fearful Tenants Stay Quiet," *McClatchy DC Bureau,* May 8, 2016, accessed March 3, 2017, http://www.mcclatchydc.com/news/nation-world/national/mcclatchys-america/article76429037.html.

He said the lady had hopped on the bus on a balmy ten degrees below zero day in Minnesota and somehow gotten turned around and was not on the right bus. She did not speak English enough to communicate with anyone, and she had no phone. Unless she bumped into another Karen person on the bus, she was in deep trouble. Finally, later on in the evening Lisa got a call; the lost lady was with the police, and they tried to sort everything out. Lisa and Eh Paw were trying to figure out which one of them should be on the phone as they communicated. Eh Paw did not feel like the authorities were understanding clearly that they needed to get an interpreter for the woman who was lost. Eh Paw said in his broken English, "It is her right. Get a translator on the phone." Eh Paw, who is usually a pretty passive guy, knew the ripple effects of being powerless and unable to communicate. He spoke up for justice when it mattered the most. The lost woman returned safely home within the next half hour.

Justice for the Captives and the Captors

I have been at this urban mission thing for a minute now, and the conversation on the topic of justice is maddening. I was once sitting with a newer church plant in a Midwestern city whose congregation was predominantly white. Their neighborhood was white and intellectual but there was a high-crime, impoverished, and mostly African-American neighborhood almost in eyeshot of their church building. About fifteen people were gathering and the church felt like they wanted to do something to engage with this neighboring, neglected community.

The justice debate started. Some were saying that they should just get in there, serve, love, and help in any practical way they could. A very intellectual woman chimed in that they shouldn't do that. The church needed to confront the systemic issues and address the powers that be to go about bringing transformation. In the end, the result was what the result often is on the justice issue. Nothing. No one did anything and injustice prevailed. Somehow, we in the city have to get a hold of the Jesus of justice enough to believe that he truly has sent us to free the captives. He truly does want liberty for both the captive and captor. There are those who are on the margins that need someone to speak for them as they have been stripped of their rights. They need a voice; their very presence is not visible to most. Then there are higher powers that continue to hold people in slavery in our world. Those systems, organizations, and processes too have to be redeemed. Organizations or groups of people are not just entities. "I'm mad at the church; I don't trust it" will not work. The church is people. Mission organizations are people. The Karen, the Somali, the Nepali—these are individual people. Captors and captives represent one life. One life at a time must be released through the justice of Jesus and that justice is declared as we live in Christlikeness in our cities. Remember Christ's words afresh as we capture his image of Kingdom liberty.

Capture His Image

The Kingdom of God has come to our cities. It may not feel like it at times; the problems feel overwhelming; the systemic injustice often feels like it never relents. Still, the Kingdom has come. Christ has us in our neighborhoods to declare his justice to those who cannot speak for themselves as well as to address the powers of our day that enslave many. The task of this section in all of this book's chapters is to come up with solutions and God-inspired actions as we move forward. This particular issue of injustice, however, can often feel heavier than others. Let us seek the Lord together as we imagine Christ's renewed vision for our neighborhood. We'll start with the micro, the one person in need of justice, and move outward.

Who in your community is experiencing injustice? How so?

What are some practical ways that you can love those who are enslaved in your community? Give a few examples.

Retell the story of the Good Samaritan in your context.

Who is the priest?

Who is the Levite?

The Samaritan?

The beaten down stranger?

What is your dangerous road to Jericho?

In declaring justice, it is essential to go after the systemic issues that keep people marginalized and alone. Jesus took the institutions head-on while sometimes stirring up much controversy. A prophetic voice is needed to speak on behalf of those who have no voice in the name of God. Further, those doing the oppressing must be confronted. Let's dive into the larger issues as we discuss.

What institutions and powers are holding people captive in your neighborhood? By what means?

What kinds of conversations need to be had with the institutions causing the injustice? What are some ideas for how a conversation should be started with these hard hitters in your community?

If the captors of injustice are not interested in having a conversation in regard to mercy or justice, what should you do next? How do you declare justice if the captors will not release the captives?

Who are the allies in your community who would be willing to join you in this fight for justice? How could you rally together around a common cause? What would that cause be?

Perhaps one of the greatest challenges in reflecting Jesus in justice is to do so with Christlikeness. I remember a young woman walking up to the academic dean of my Bible college in the late nineties telling him how angry she was. She made sure he knew that the anger she had was righteous. In declaring justice, a true prophetic voice from the Spirit needs not our own endorsement of righteousness. Justice comes with salvation bringing healing and restoration for all at our city's gates. Obviously, this is easier said than done, but a prophetic voice heals. Justice brings life and renewal. We would do well to take this posture in reflecting Jesus in justice. Discuss the remaining questions in regard to our posture as we combat injustice.

What examples of prophetic voices inside or outside of your community have you witnessed? Have those voices been helpful or harmful? How so?

What can we learn from Jesus' actions in turning the tables over in the temple? What was his chief concern, and why did people listen to him?

In empowering those from the ethnic community to do ministry within the city, what changes should be made? What models can be applied to ensure that ministry and urban mission is a level playing field for all to participate?

Take a moment and ask the Holy Spirit what needs to be said and what needs to be done to combat injustice in your city. Write down what the Spirit drops in your heart. Share with your ministry team as you close the discussion.

Jesus loved the one whom the rest of the world thought was invisible. He loved them without limit. With one arm around the marginalized, he had a whip in the other hand chasing away institutional powers that kept the individual bound. We too are called to follow his example. Living on mission takes on these issues toe to toe, and we lay those burdens at the feet of Christ. It has always been and always will be his liberating power that will bring freedom. Bitterness and anger rooted in the hostility of the enemy cannot be the driving force of justice. The reign of God wherein his joy races through the streets is the fulfillment of justice being displayed in the city. Pray with me as Amos cried out, "But let justice roll on like a river, righteousness like a never-failing stream!

Chapter 9
REFLECTING HIS IMAGE IN COMMUNITY

Zoom-In

The Word became flesh and made his dwelling among us. We have seen his glory, the glory of the one and only Son, who came from the Father, full of grace and truth. (John 1:14)

When one of those at the table with him heard this, he said to Jesus, "Blessed is the one who will eat at the feast in the kingdom of God."

Jesus replied: "A certain man was preparing a great banquet and invited many guests. At the time of the banquet he sent his servant to tell those who had been invited, 'Come, for everything is now ready.'

"But they all alike began to make excuses. The first said, 'I have just bought a field, and I must go and see it. Please excuse me.'

"Another said, 'I have just bought five yoke of oxen, and I'm on my way to try them out. Please excuse me.'

"Still another said, 'I just got married, so I can't come.'

"The servant came back and reported this to his master. Then the owner of the house became angry and ordered his servant, 'Go out quickly into the streets and alleys of the town and bring in the poor, the crippled, the blind and the lame.'

"'Sir,' the servant said, 'what you ordered has been done, but there is still room.'

"Then the master told his servant, 'Go out to the roads and country lanes and compel them to come in, so that my house will be full. I tell you, not one of those who were invited will get a taste of my banquet.'" (Luke 14:15-24)

Jesus continually found his way into a good party and entered fully into the life of the community around him. These circumstances were certainly not ideal for a religious person, much less the Messiah, but he weaves his way in and out of celebrations throughout the Gospels. In Luke 15:2 we find Jesus being carefully watched by the elite of society because he associated with sinners. The context of this text comes alongside multiple examples where Jesus is found associating with community members that the religious leaders did not approve of, and he was chastised for such fellowship. In Matthew 9:9-13, Christ calls Matthew the tax collector to him as he is reclining at a table amongst other tax collectors and is promptly criticized for his actions. Further, we find the term "friend of sinners" being raised from Matthew 11:16-19 and Luke 7:30-35 as an insult because of Christ's choice to socialize with the "wrong" group of people according to the religious. When a sinful woman anoints Christ's feet with expensive perfume and dries them with her hair, the crowd again becomes hostile towards this demonstration of grace in community (Luke 7:36-50). Over and over again, the people who kept religious order were upset that Christ dined in the homes of those who were on the outskirts of society (Luke 15:1-2; 19:1-10).

At every turn, Jesus can be found participating in the community amongst those who most need salvation.[137]

All are Invited to the Party

In telling the Parable of the Great Banquet, Jesus implies that the reign of God is characterized by having joy, by dancing, by celebrating, and by feasting.[138] Honored guests would know about such a banquet well in advance and in excusing themselves with little regret demonstrates that they do not know the significance of such an event. Just as Israel had long awaited the coming Messiah who is now inaugurating his Kingdom, they find themselves too busy to participate in the glorious day.[139] Excuses, rejection, and preoccupation—all of these and more are given explaining Israel's colossal failure to enter the banquet.

Bailey explains the cultural nuances of buying a field, obtaining oxen, and getting married as these are the three excuses given by the guest. The manner in which the guests excuse themselves would have been most disrespectful according to Middle Eastern culture, and, in all of these examples, they would

---

137. Kevin DeYoung, "Jesus Friend of Sinners, but How?" *The Gospel Coalition,* March 4, 2014, accessed March 14, 2017, https://blogs.thegospelcoalition.org/kevindeyoung/2014/03/04/jesus-friend-of-sinners-but-how/. DeYoung highlights Jesus' interaction with sinners in this sampling of passages emphasizing that Christ does not associate with such people just to make a shocking statement nor should this be ground for us flippantly saying, "Jesus hung out with drunk people all the time." The point is that he aggressively announces his Kingdom in the context of relationship associating with those who most need salvation.

138. Takatemjen, "Luke" in *South Asia Bible Commentary,* ed. Brian Wintle (Grand Rapids, MI: Zondervan Publishing, 2015), 1364.

139. Wright, *Luke for Everyone,* 177.

have known about their acquiring of possessions and marriage far in advance. If all of the guests refuse, the banquet could not go on.[140] But Jesus, both the King of community and Merciful Servant, turns the anger the host felt into grace. He tells his servant to quickly go and invite the disabled and those at the bottom of the pile to come be invited in. He wants his house to be full and the party enjoyed. A grace-filled community characterizes Christlike mission and is true once more in the context of a community party.

Jesus Came Full of Grace and Truth

Pohl describes the biblical concept of living in the truth as being inextricably tied to the idea of "faithfulness and reliability."[141] In the words, sentences, and teachings of Scripture, we have an unchanging truth that is eternal and sharper than a double-edged sword (Heb. 4:12). Jesus embodies such truth even when he was in the most difficult of situations at dinner parties with mixed audiences. To the philosophers and theologians of his day, the concept of the Word becoming flesh would have been an impossible conception to make.[142] This reality could most visibly be expressed in the context of relationships in the community. We see the grace-truth character of Christ so clearly in this parable as the master responds to his anger by compelling more people and the lowest sector of society at that to be invited into his banquet.

---

140. Kenneth Bailey, *Jesus through Middle Eastern Eyes* (Downers Grove, IL: InterVarsity Press, 2007), 315-317.

141. Christine Pohl, *Living Into Community: Cultivating Practices That Sustain Us* (Grand Rapids, MI: Eerdmans Publishing, 2012), Kindle Location 2708.

142. Keener, Kindle Location 13393.

Jesus is reliable, faithful, full of grace, full of truth. The grace-filled life is one that invites, includes, and compels the community to participate in God's Kingdom party.

For Jesus, being full of the truth did not necessitate that he flee from controversy or stay out of spheres where he could be falsely accused. Quite the contrary, Jesus stayed glued to the fabric of his society giving himself one opportunity after another to announce the Kingdom. In the temple, in homes, on the side of the road, on the shores of the sea—wherever there were people gathered, Jesus was present showing grace and truth.

Urban Theology of Place

Ray Bakke reminds us that reflecting Jesus in community cannot be disconnected from the places which contain great issues of power, race, wealth, and ethnicity.[143] To move along in our witness and ministry in the urban context and to ignore these realities reflect a Jesus who has not fully come into focus. Community life has a myriad of issues around wealth, justice, inequality, and race, many of which Jesus addressed head-on and which are being raised throughout this text. Bakke further pushes us to begin to embrace a theology of sacred spaces. Everywhere Jesus goes is Bethel, the house of God. When Jesus became grace and truth and gave a Kingdom party invitation for the community, he was not merely expanding his reach on the places he was influencing. No, Jesus transformed every place he trod. Bakke writes, "Every ghetto I have been to has at least one believer there.

---

143. Bakke, *A Theology as Big as the City*, Kindle Location 1239.

It's not a bad neighborhood. The place you are standing on is holy ground."[144]

The setting of the great banquet would have likely included a time for an important matter of the day to be discussed. Religion and political discourse were common at such events.[145] The social issues of our time are not peripheral issues to community; rather, they define the quality of life for those around us. Just as Jesus modeled in his life in the community, we must choose when and how to speak to most visibly reflect the Kingdom of God and address the issues of our day. Tense moments during a community gathering is no time to retreat to the kitchen and grab another slice of pizza, for a conversation of salvation, justice, equality, or freedom may need to be had.

Eating Together in God's Kingdom

Christine Pohl has connected in a profound way what takes place spiritually as we eat together. Signs and echoes of the Kingdom resound through her words:

Eating together, ritualized in the Lord's Supper, continually reenacts the center of the gospel. As we remember the cost of our welcome, Christ's broken body and shed blood, we also celebrate the reconciliation and relationship available to us through his sacrifice and through his hospitality. In that sacrament, we are nourished on our journey towards God's

---

144. Bakke, *A Theology As Big as the City,"* Kindle Location 1239-40.

145. Bailey, 308-09.

banquet table even as we experience the present joy and welcome associated with sharing in that table.[146]

Jesus' Parable of the Great Banquet puts feasting as the centerpiece, bringing people together far and wide. Christ further shows his disciples the intimacy in sharing a meal with them in his last moments on earth reminding them of his eventual sacrifice and suffering. There is something divinely beautiful about sharing a meal together whether it is for the purpose of communion or party. As Pohl reminds us, perhaps the activity closest to the Kingdom of God is eating together.[147]

The Nepali word for the Lord's Supper or community is simply translated "The Lord's Party" (*Prabu boj*). This simple translation has a powerful ring to it when placed in the context of the great banquet. The King of the earth has laid a table before us with an invitation to commune with him and other believers. As we gather together in community, there is no other way to describe the event other than God's party of grace, mercy, reconciliation, and welcome. The party could literally be a feast with hundreds of people from our neighborhood; it may be a knock at the door at 10:00 p.m., and our neighbor is turning towards us in brokenness. It may be a tragic night or one filled with hope. The Spirit's work in community flows like water taking shape to fill each season and circumstance. All are invited. All are honored guests.

---

146. Christine Pohl, *Making Room: Rediscovering Hospitality as a Christian Tradition* (Grand Rapids, MI: Eerdmans Publishing, 1999), Kindle Location 379-80.

147. Ibid., Kindle Location 380-81.

Zoom-Out

"The best testimony of the truth of the gospel is the quality of our lives together. Jesus risked his reputation and the credibility of his story by tying them to how his followers lived and cared for one another in community (John 17:20-23)."[148] – Christine Pohl

During our Minneapolis-St. Paul days, one of my fondest memories was the picnics we used to have across the street from our apartment at McCarron's Park. Minnesota winters mean that anytime it warms up enough to get outdoors, you do it. It was not uncommon for our little church to invite a bunch of our friends to a picnic on a whim. Wednesday nights, Sunday afternoons, and Friday nights—whenever we had a moment, we'd grab the community and get together. Anywhere from eight to thirty people would run to the store, get what we needed, and celebrate. Celebrate what? Nothing really, yet everything. The Kingdom of God had come and to see Buddhist, Hindu, and Christian neighbors come together from various socio-cultural backgrounds was food to the soul. Nothing can compare to that sense of belonging and that season of our lives is forever frozen in our memories.

For those of us who have tasted the community of the King, we have a hard time returning to life as usual. The closeness that comes with sharing our lives together is unlike any experience most of us have ever known. From Fresno, to Chicago, Minneapolis, and Pittsburgh, these kinds of parties run in between the lines of this book and the immigrant community with its festive way of life leaving a mark on city sidewalks, apartment courtyards, and parks throughout America. I wish I had an audio

---

148. Pohl, *Living Into Community*, Kindle Location 61-62.

recording to send you when I call friends and colleagues in their neighborhoods. Every time I call, it seems that I hear a party happening on the other side of the phone. People are just hanging at an apartment, walking down the street, shouting from their porch—this life in the city is foreign to so many.

Paco and Little Village

Paco, Chris's pastor in Little Village in Chicago, was reminiscing on his early days in the neighborhood where he used to just pop in at a neighbor's house and basically invite himself over for a meal. Living in Little Village for twenty years now, with thirteen of those years pastoring a church, things have changed significantly. Paco remembers about two years ago when he and his leadership team had a defining moment when they knew they needed to return to the practice of visiting folks in their homes and getting off their own turf. He remembers that nearly all of his meetings with people were happening at the church or at a local coffee shop, ensuring that most of his interaction would happen outside of the homes of neighbors.[149]

One Sunday Paco committed to plowing through this realization and walked up to a guy who had been attending his church for some time but had not really made much commitment to Christ or his family. He told Aniseto, his newer congregant, that he would be coming to his house on Tuesday evening. In response, Aniseto simply wrote down his address and gave it to Paco. As promised, Paco showed up on Tuesday night, and it was no small gathering. Relatives and co-workers from the neighborhood were

---

149. Paco Amador, "Christianity's Most Vivid Celebration is a Meal," *Christianity Today*, March 2, 2017, accessed March 14, 2017, http://www.christianitytoday.com/edstetzer/2017/february/christianitys-most-vivid-celebration-is-meal.html.

there, and the night was naturally centered around food. Paco began to share the gospel as the group ate, laughed, and talked together. Paco asked Aniseto, "What would stop you from opening your heart to Jesus right here and now?"

Aniseto responded, "Nothing. I have been waiting for someone to ask me this."[150]

A couple weeks after that, Aniseto was baptized at a community block party before a large crowd in the neighborhood.

In the weeks and months following, Aniseto has been introducing about one person a month to the Lord. The newfound commitments are followed up in baptism. The entire trajectory of Aniseto's home and many homes in the community all started around the dinner table. The anxiety that Paco felt as he knocked on Aniseto's door is a distant memory now as the community of Jesus is being displayed with visible power. Paco's humility is a lesson to all of us that God still has work for us to do. Even in the most communal, inviting neighborhoods of our country we can easily put it on cruise control and coast throughout the day. The Holy Spirit's conviction upon Paco and a group of friends stirred their hearts afresh towards evangelism and that Kingdom party is now being evidenced through inviting themselves over to neighbors' homes.

The Community Break Up

Parties are one thing, but the daily grind of dealing with sharing life together is a different story altogether. Inevitably there will be conflict, pain, even fallout. When Jesus incarnated the Word of God, he came full of grace and truth. In order to truly

---

150. Ibid.

practice community that includes all stages of family life, we will have to continually learn to walk in that balance of grace and truth. We can all likely remember a time of loss in regard to community. A relationship break up, a pastor moving on, theological or personality schisms, rejection in relationships that were once strong but had become less than ideal—these sorts of losses are common and can alter the way we live in community causing many of us to never take risks ever again.

In 2013, I announced to our church, the same folks that we used to do all the spontaneous picnics with, that we would be stepping away to take a new assignment in Nepal. I believed that I had prepared the church well, and we had enough core people there to walk through the transition and come out better on the other side. I was wrong. A handful of core people left our small church as they relocated to be near family. The bond of closeness that we all had with one another was apparently tied closer to my wife and me as the leaders than we originally expected. In the weeks and months following, relational, theological, and leadership disconnect erupted and the ship sank. Without strong leadership, congruence in theology, and strong relational bond, there was no other choice but to disband.

This community break up has affected me and many involved in ways I never imagined. Unintentionally, I offended people. I was offended. We have had various long conversations with different members of the community, and it has taken a long time to restore some of that pain. No one woke up and decided to pick apart the strong bond of community that was there. Circumstances, emotions, opinions, and personalities all contributed to a perfect storm. Certainly, we have all learned better paths forward when it comes to a transition such as this, but we still don't know how smoothly things will go in the future as we risk again. This season for all of us was an extremely difficult one and a memory that still causes my chest to tighten as I reflect upon it. Pain and loss in community are some of the more challenging things we will face in urban work or in life in any context for that matter.

Fresno Community Meal

Nancy recounts one of the foundational pieces to ministry in Fresno as being a group of missionaries who get together for food, fellowship, and prayer every Sunday evening. Several years ago, an urban leader in her community decided that this was a good, Godward thing to do, and they have been meeting weekly for over fifteen years now. She says that every once in a while the group of fifteen to thirty starts waning, but someone always rises up and pushes the commitment to community forward. It has been an integral part of Nancy's sixteen years in Fresno and a commitment that she would not want to let slip from her grasp.

Urban workers need a community of people that will hold them accountable, encourage them in the life of God, and pray with them consistently. The example of Fresno stands out as it is one that has survived the test of time. A pastor friend of mine in St. Paul, Jim Olson, has had a similar commitment with two or three local pastors where they sit, talk, and pray together one morning per week. The community that Christ has formed all around us is integral not only to the integrity of the gospel message but also to its messengers. Without community, there is no mission.

Nepali Believers in the Midst of Hindu Society

In the last seven years, the experience for many of our Nepali neighbors has changed dramatically as they have come out of Hinduism to embrace Jesus. All of Nepali society revolves around Hindu celebrations throughout the year wherein relatives, friends, and even those abroad come back to visit. It cannot be over-communicated how much celebrations, festivals, and family gatherings are part of the society. When many of our neighbors began to come to the Lord, however, this created a great deal of tension because the very celebrations that they had come to appreciate and enjoy were suddenly realized to be the roots of Hinduism, idol worship, and the lies that they are now rejecting. A choice to not participate in these celebrations is a very conscious decision to cut oneself off from the broader Hindu community. Just last week as I was sitting with my neighbor Hem, he was telling me about the difficulty of navigating through all of these things.

There is pressure from the Christian community to reject certain things: not attend Hindu weddings, funerals, or holiday celebrations. Hindus would also likely feel a bit of this tension in reverse as they would be some of the few Hindus in the midst of Christian celebrations when they come to Christian gatherings. What inevitably ends up happening is that these two communities isolate themselves from one another and only casual encounters are made. The cross alone, not cultural schisms, should be a stumbling block for those who do not believe (1 Cor. 1:23), but we have to admit that complete disengagement is not the answer, and we can improve in our practice of community with those different from us.

Reflecting Jesus in the city means that we form a community of believers where all are welcome and belong. Community becomes the ultimate test for transformation. If we cannot figure out how to get along with each other, engage with the community around us, and continually grow to be more like Christ, the whole thing is over. The mission is aborted. Careful attention to community life is imperative, and the positive results of a community that reflects Christ in all they say and do has no comparison under heaven. The disciples who met with and walked with Jesus were undone as they encountered a Kingdom community. Such a family created in Christ rolled on long after Christ's ascension and fueled the practice of the early Church.

We fix our gaze again on John 1 . . . Jesus moved into the neighborhood, full of grace and truth, as Eugene Peterson translated. Though neighborhoods have changed considerably and our urban context may be far from first-century Palestine, the need for community has not changed. This phrase "grace and truth" becomes an incredibly important phrase as we apply Scripture. Jesus knew how to walk back and forth between dicey situations in community and models well for us how to live with one another. Let the Spirit bring to memory the parties and the pain in your neighborhood as you focus on God's renewed vision for your community.

Capture His Image

Opening our homes and entering into the homes of others in our neighborhoods is the slow, steady grind of seeing God's Kingdom community demonstrated in power. The silence during times of mourning, the laughter during a birthday party, the continual unannounced visits can all be potential times for the Spirit to work and be ever present. Jesus came into the world, full of grace and truth, not withholding or pulling back in terms of vulnerability, trust, and time investment. We stand at the gates of our community with the doors open wide, and we must decide if we will enter. Too many urban workers have stood afar off, never entering fully into the lives of those around them, short-circuiting the Kingdom community Jesus came to bring. Let us think honestly and dialogue with openness as we discuss our practice of reflecting Jesus in community.

What is the equivalent of the great banquet in your community? Who are the elite? Who are those on the outskirts of the community that we need to compel to join the party?

What excuses do you feel that those in your community are making for not participating in the banquet before them?

What are the barriers that stand in your way as you seek to engage in your community? How can you overcome such barriers?

Jesus raised difficult issues at the parties he attended. What are some of the issues the Holy Spirit may be asking you to discuss at social gatherings in your community?

Is your view of practicing Christian community tied to salvation being offered to those who are gathered in popular social spaces throughout the neighborhood?

As discussed at the opening of the chapter, practicing authentic community can be costly and even painful. Yet, it is the practice of Christ's people living together which is the most visible sign to the world that the message and reality of God are true. It seems that many ministries and churches want to skirt around the difficulties of sharing life together. Closing our eyes will not make the challenges go away. Reflecting Jesus amongst hurting people is hard. Urban workers though who can stay the course and hang in there with one another will be able to reap the reward of sacrificial love if they simply stay in the game and refuse to bow out when things get difficult. Emotional and social friction is inevitable. Let's discuss the challenges and tasks before us.

Can you share an experience where the community you were part of was disbanded? What things distracted them and caused the mission to be aborted?

Name two or three practices in community life that have helped you stay in good relationship over the long haul. How have they helped you?

Give examples of "grace and truth" in the context of your church or ministry. How are you presently showing grace and truth? How have you shown so in the past?

Whose house do you need to invite yourself over to? What do you feel the Spirit may be saying to you about this invitation?

Is hospitality driving your life personally or your ministry corporately? How so? Give specific examples.

Reflecting Jesus in the city is not a calling that is done in isolation. God has called the Church, who is his community, to mirror to the world his rule and reign. When Jesus prayed that his Kingdom would come on the earth as it is in heaven, such a coming cannot take place outside of community. Americans are some of the most rugged, individualistic people on the planet. We often live hours from immediate relatives, and our correspondence can be infrequent. Every man for himself is a mantra that we like to tout around as if it were the gospel. It is not.

The gospel of the Kingdom is that Jesus likens his reign to a great banquet where all are welcome and all are invited. We do everything possible to extend the invitation to all people regardless of their status or influence. Though the struggles are immense and living in deep relationship with each other always means high commitment, we cannot choose to retreat when challenging times surface. Practicing grace and truth is so essential as we walk with our neighbors knowing that we need the same kind of life that Christ himself established in community. The Spirit has not given us a spirit of timidity but one of power, love, and self-discipline (2 Tim. 1:7). Just as Jesus knew how to stay present in community and thrived in the process, may we learn to offer hope and salvation as we engage daily in our cities.

Chapter 10
REFLECTING HIS IMAGE IN UNITY

Zoom-In

"My prayer is not for them alone. I pray also for those who will believe in me through their message, that all of them may be one, Father, just as you are in me and I am in you. May they also be in us so that the world may believe that you have sent me. I have given them the glory that you gave me, that they may be one as we are one—I in them and you in me—so that they may be brought to complete unity. Then the world will know that you sent me and have loved them even as you have loved me." (John 17:20-23)

The word picture we gain from this final prayer before Jesus goes to the cross is awe-inspiring. Jesus, in the last moments before his death, is not among the crowds. He is not drafting up plan B, C, or D for when the disciples will inevitably veer off course upon his exit. Jesus is alone with the disciples. Praying. To what degree Christ is reflecting on what is to come, we do not know. What is clear in this beautiful image, however, is that Jesus was thinking of the future generations and how this gospel would be placed in the hands of those who would remain once he returned to the Father. Disciple after disciple would carry this prayer to the city. To the village. To the stranger. To a friend. Christ in his final moments on earth prayed for us. This prayer of unity mirrors the

Trinity God we worship. The epistles to be written later would echo this longing Christ had for his followers. The death and resurrection Jesus was about to face, and the eventual pouring out of the Spirit hinge on the kind of love that will be shown through Christlike unity.[151]

Unity in Passing on the Gospel

N. T. Wright contrasts reading verses 20 and 21 of John 17 to a historian who picks up a copy of Shakespeare, Plato, or Socrates and suddenly finds a section in the manuscript where the author is talking directly to him.[152] This is precisely what is happening with the prayer of Jesus. He is praying for us with the desire that the world would believe in the message of the cross in the way that unity is displayed among us. The prayer assumes a commitment to unity, but it also assumes an expectation that the gospel will be carried to the future generations. Considering Matthew 28 and Acts 1:8, this unifying prayer is connected to the mission of God that will cross cultural, economic, and language barriers in order that the gospel be planted in the hearts of those who have not yet understood it.

The incarnation embodies the mission of Christ and ensures the exaltation of the Father is made known. The prayer of unity here again reflects Jesus' mission that the world will believe the message we preach. While love and unity is the evidence of our

---

151. Dave Jenkins, "The Work and Person of the Holy Spirit in the Gospel of John," *Blue Letter Bible,* March 5, 2013, accessed March 22, 2017, http://blogs.blueletterbible.org/blb/2013/03/05/the-work-and-person-of-the-holy-spirit-in-the-gospel-of-john/. He emphasizes the glorification of Christ being essential to the message and mission of Jesus. To not be glorified would not fulfill Scripture nor his Father's will.

152. N.T. Wright, *John for Everyone: Part 2 Chapters 11-21,* (Louisville, KY: John Knox Press, 2002), 98.

message, Jesus' prayer insinuates that we will announce his teachings and stories to generations of all the nations. In praying for "those who will believe," Jesus prays in faith that the message of the gospel will take root in the lives and hearts of the people with whom we share. Whether this message be passed on to those in a local, monocultural context or it travels to a city with extremely complex socio-cultural dynamics, the call is for the message to be proclaimed and believed.

Unity and the City

John's readers would hear this prayer with gravity as religious and ethnic turmoil was in their midst. Some of the early Christians were ousted from the synagogue, and Jewish colleagues had returned to the synagogue making pronouncements that Jesus was not the Messiah.[153] False teaching centered around idolatry in Smyrna and Ephesus. Both cities were undergoing such strain. Ephesus had dispelled the false teachers but were disunified. At best, false teaching and idolatry were issues raised but full-blown Gnosticism denying the incarnation was likely.[154] Christians would be a very small minority in a world with values quite unlike Christ introduced in announcing the Kingdom of God.

Relational, theological, and ethnic tensions were felt by the readers of the Gospel of John as well as his epistles. Each city was dealing with varying levels of disunity, and the prayer Jesus prayed would resonate in hearts and minds. Cities regardless of time and place have many of the same realities as did the first century. Disparate views on God and humanity produce

---

153. Keener, Kindle Location 13393.

154. Keener, Kindle Location 13392-4.

environments that make the call to unity a real challenge. The Roman government as well as Alexander the Great's views of oneness and unifying of humanity would have been understood in first-century times, but the kind of unity Christ embodied would have been altogether different.[155] The contrast is striking as the oneness that he calls for is rooted in love and mercy not power or force.

False teaching, idolatry, racial tension, betrayal—all the issues and more that disrupted the early Church to whom John was writing bear such similarity into American cities. The Church often struggles to have a voice amongst the plethora of opinions that fill our streets. Newly arrived Christ-following immigrants have often asked me where all the believers are in the city as the picture they are receiving from urban America is older white folks hanging on to church life in ethnic neighborhoods. The unity Jesus prayed for does not exist in a hole in the ground merely speaking to a subculture of do-gooders. The gospel of the Kingdom unified in love speaks to the urban situation and circumstance. To a city divided, the reflection of Christ is Good News.

Love and Glory

The love of God is the continual display to the world that Jesus is the Messiah; his glory is visibly expressed in love through

---

155. Rodney A. Whitacre, "Jesus Concludes His Time with His Disciples By Praying to His Father," *IVP New Testament Commentary Series: John,* vol. 4. , ed. Grant R. Osborne (Downers Grove, IL: IVP Academic, 2010), accessed March 20, 2017, https://www.biblegateway.com/resources/commentaries/IVP-NT/John/Jesus-Concludes-Time-Alone.IVP Commentary.

Christ's going to the cross.[156] The glory of God could not be revealed any other way. By living in God's unity with others, we glorify Jesus to all who witness such love. The command of Christ to love the Lord your God with all your heart, soul, mind, and strength (Mark 12:30) is the same thrust in his unifying prayer. With everything inside of us, the community of the King is to visibly reflect the love of Christ while giving glory to God.

Some have struggled with the concept of the Father giving glory to Christ as if to suggest there is some sort of arrogance within Jesus in making such a statement. To not be supreme and to not be glorified, however, is the antithesis of the gospel message. If he is not supreme, he is not worthy of worship. Christ died. Christ rose. That resurrection was rooted in compassionate suffering and thus his exaltation of glory. These are not just lofty, nice sounding words. As we are unified with one another, bearing witness to Christ, this same love and glory of Jesus is known to the world.[157] There can be no denying that Christ is who he said he was if his followers reflect his love to those all around them.

Complete Unity

Christ's prayer is for complete unity, a unity that echoes none other than the Father and the Son. The letters of Ephesians and Galatians highlight that the cross has broken down every

---

156. D.A. Carson, "*The Supremacy of Christ and Love in a Postmodern World*" (message, Desiring God 2006 National Conference, September 30, 2006), accessed March 21, 2017, http://www.desiringgod.org/messages/the-supremacy-of-christ-and-love-in-a-postmodern-world

157. Jonathan Parnell, "One Way to Glory in the Cross," *Desiring God,* November 28, 2011, accessed March 21, 2017, http://www.desiringgod.org/articles/one-way-to-glory-in-the-cross. Parnell emphasizes that one of the most beautiful displays of Christ's glory, his death and resurrection, is the reconciling of ethnic groups worshipping together.

barrier: the wall of hostility that existed between Jew and Greek, slave and free, male and female (Gal. 3:28; Eph. 2:14). The prayer of unity is not something that we manufacture but is something that was accomplished through the redemption of Christ. This completeness of unity that Jesus prayed for reflects the relationship of God the Father and Jesus himself. Trying to get at the heart of Jesus' final prayer is quite the task as everything in the incarnation is summed up here. There is mission, there is love, glory, the Trinity God, disciple-making, a reminder that Jesus will leave, the promise of the cross and resurrection. It is all here, and the complete unity prayed for is one where purpose, mission, surrender, love, and glory are firmly established in Christ's Church.

In this final prayer of Jesus, the different pieces of His life come full circle to be a pure reflection of divine grace and truth. Prayer, mission, suffering, discipleship, compassion, humility, family, justice, community—the complete unity of Christ's body is displayed to the city as we bring these all together. While what lies before us may seem daunting, and the road to unity unachievable, let us remind ourselves that the Spirit of the living God fills our lives and can fill our cities with his glory. This has always been and will always be the plan for the Word becoming flesh, the Kingdom of God reigning in our midst. Pause and pray this prayer alone before moving into the contemporary scene and reflection.

Zoom-Out

Jesus prayed that we would be one just as he and the Father are one. That call and cry for unity would become the sign to the world that he was the Messiah and had truly been sent. As we survey churches in America, even churches in contexts which are ethnically diverse, we find the struggle to obey the command of Christ. Division theologically, racially, economically, and linguistically is a common thread that weaves its way through our city blocks.

The latest research has shown that as our nation increases in diversity, our churches are not really shifting gears with roughly 90% of congregations being monocultural.[158] Social sciences have shown that as we spend excessive time with our "in-group" we increasingly bond around our sameness, and anyone who is different from us becomes more and more of an outsider. We can easily vilify people merely for being different from us creating polarization that may be completely false or unnecessary.[159]

These polarizations were perhaps no more visible during the 2016 political season wherein many Christians have vowed to disassociate themselves with the evangelical label due to thousands of believers voting for Donald Trump.[160]

Christena Cleveland describes rightly in her book that we have firmly established the view of "right Christian" and "wrong Christian" in our minds.[161] Pro-choice/pro-life, liberal/conservative, black lives matter/all lives matter,

---

158. Michael O. Emerson and Christian Smith, *Divided By Faith: Evangelical Religion and the Problem of Race in America* (New York: Oxford University Press, 2000), 28-30.

159. Christena Cleveland, Disunity in Christ: Uncovering the Hidden Forces That Keep Us Apart (Downers Grove, IL: IVP, 2013), 27.

160. Kyle Rohane, "Are Pastors Discarding the Evangelical Label?," *Christianity Today,* November 2016, accessed March 19, 2017, http://www.christianitytoday.com/pastors/2016/november-web-exclusives/are-evangelical-pastors-discarding-evangelical-label.html.

161. Cleveland, 12.

immigration reform/send them all back, transgender bathrooms/no transgender bathrooms, refugee ban/no refugee ban—the list goes on and on and believers on both sides of these issues reside in our communities. There is no question that the urban context often produces a certain slant on political positioning, but there is no one size fits all for any of these issues. The media and technology no longer seclude us from each other and often people know where we stand. Still, the call of unity remains and Jesus' words to be one as he and the Father are one is the cry of the Church.

St. Paul Bethel Christian Fellowship

Pastor Jim Olson came to Bethel Christian Fellowship twenty years ago to a small congregation in the heart of the city in St. Paul, MN. The Twin Cities is a very diverse place with the St. Paul Public School System now having more than 129 languages represented in the homes of its students.[162] The surrounding neighborhoods have grown to be African, Asian, and Hispanic as well as Caucasian and African-American living in mixed communities. Little by little, the church began to visibly reflect their neighborhood and made a deliberate attempt to do so. Today, the church has Haitian, Karen (of Burma), and Nepali congregations as well as a significant outreach to the Somali Muslim community in their midst. Several years ago, Pastor Jim completed his Doctor of Ministry wherein he focused on intercultural church ministry as the major theme. It has not been without time, study, and labor that this pathway was pursued.

---

162. St. Paul Public Schools Office of Multilingual Learning, "SPPS EL Facts," accessed March 23, 2017, http://spps.schoolwires.net/Domain/10453.

I was sitting with the youth pastor, Ben Clark, some years ago and he talked about the transition that his youth group experienced during this shift: language challenges, cultural differences, even religious divisions as kids came from Hindu and Buddhist backgrounds to the church. During our coffee meeting that day, Ben described an international night where groups of students from different countries presented their cultural flavor of the gospel so each person in the youth group could greater appreciate where one another had come from. Internship programs, multi-ethnic worship, ESL Alpha classes—these and so much more are being done under unified leadership committed to Jesus' vision for a diverse community of worshippers.

Bethel Christian Fellowship continually makes attempts such as these to bridge the cultural divide and is one of the best examples I have seen in economic, racial, and academic unity in the body of Christ. Still, nothing is easy. Nepalis with little English may be hovering together in the back of the sanctuary during a joint service as majority culture folks do not have the language to interact with them. Nothing this side of heaven is perfect, but they plow ahead understanding that their church must be a house of prayer for all nations.[163]

The Challenge of Unity in First-Generation Immigrant Churches

Over the last decade, our family has had the privilege of working with first-generation immigrant churches, most of which

---

163. Bethel Christian Fellowship, "About Us, Our Calling," accessed March 23, 2017, http://betheltwincities.org/who-we-are/our-calling. The church's mission is to "radiate joy as a house of prayer for all nations." As I have talked with leadership over the years, this calling is reflected in all aspects of church life.

have been first-generation Christians. There is nothing more exhilarating than seeing the gospel take root in a culture where it has not been previously, and the passion in new believers spurs on those of us who have been following Jesus for several years. With the excitement and growth, however, is a real challenge to keep the church moving in a direction that is God-honoring, grounded, and unified.

The tendency that we have seen over the last decade in first-generation immigrant church work and elsewhere in other contexts is that oftentimes there is very little being done in the way of leadership development or training. Because of the marginalized status that many immigrants receive, the church is often a place where status can be elevated and leadership roles are given.[164] In one regard, this is empowering, but it often creates a vacuum due to inadequate preparation.

In addition, very little accountability is provided. Shallow roots with little accountability make for a disaster waiting to happen. False teaching, disunity within the church, and fear have seemed to dominate, and there is a firestorm left in its wake. Few are very willing to clean up such a mess so what continues to happen is fracture after fracture further separating the body of Christ from one another.

Recently, I talked to two different Nepali Christians who by Nepali church standards are mature in their faith. I could hear

---

164. Soong-Chan Rah, *The Next Evangelicalism: Freeing the Church From Western Cultural Captivity* (Downers Grove, IL: IVP, 2009), 175-76. Using the Korean immigrant church as a model, Soong-Chan Rah explains the marginalized status of many first-generation immigrants. The church becomes a place where status can be elevated and as high as 32% of church attendees have been given a leadership role. Both the Korean and African-American church show such findings and this rings true in my immigrant church experience as well.

the fear in their voices as they began to express their concerns about false teaching and those they care for potentially being swept away into such doctrine. A pastor with six months of Bible school training is often on the higher end of theological training and many ministry functions are simply modeled from what they have seen practiced by others, from the internet, or hearsay. It is not the immigrant churches' fault that they have come along and are new in their faith. It is a wonderful problem that there is growth happening. But the lack of training, shallow roots, and low bar of accountability presents a real landmine in terms of Christian unity.[165] Reflecting Jesus in unity demands that we stand in the gap for each other and do everything we possibly can to foster unity in Christ's name.

Praying Together in Chicago

Every Palm Sunday the streets of Little Village become a sanctuary as believers join in a march known as "Cry Chicago." People come with their families and palm branches and unite together to cry over the injustice, hopelessness, and darkness that hangs over their city. Krista in Little Village sent out an informal update amongst friends and prayer partners not many days before this march. It reads as follows:

---

165. Helen Lee, "Chapter 4: Healthy Leaders, Healthy Households," in *Growing Healthy Asian-American Churches,* ed. Peter Cha, Steve Kang, and Helen Lee (Downers Grove, IL: IVP, 2006), Kindle Location 660-64. Writing from a second-generation immigrant perspective, Helen Lee points to the cultural mishaps of false humility and saving face as being detrimental to strong leadership. Even amongst churches that have leaders who have been well trained there is often a cultural divide where seminary is for the mainstream American church and what is discussed in the classroom stays in the classroom. Disengagement combined with cultural nuances in not addressing problems can often lead to tension and fallout.

I was struck by a quote I read this morning in the *Week of Prayer for Christian Unity* devotional. "Where there is hatred, let us sow love; where there is injury, pardon; where there is doubt, faith; where there is despair, hope; where there is darkness, light; where there is sadness, joy." This week a two-year old child was killed right by my school. Just hours before a young man who has two cousins in my classroom was killed. In November their uncle was killed. In September their aunt died of an overdose. The need is overwhelming! God's calling is huge in the midst of a broken world, but He who calls us is even greater. Let us be light in this dark, broken world![166]

When believers and churches unite amid their community of 90,000 and the voice of Christ-followers becomes louder than the cries of the atrocities in the neighborhood, it is noticed. The highest teen pregnancy rate of any high school in the state, undocumented folks being scared out of their minds under the new US government administration, businesses posing as legit companies which are actually drug covers, rampant gang violence—when the church unites, these injustices are pushed back and Christ is lifted high. In joining together in unifying prayer as Little Village believers walk down the community's busiest streets, they are praying along with Krista that the light truly will be brighter than the darkness. Chris has remarked that this symbol of unity and the tears being shed during "Cry Chicago" is a sight to behold. The Kingdom of God has broken into Little Village and it is being demonstrated in Christ-exalting unity.

We opened this book by considering the life of Jesus through surveying his commitment to prayer and rest. It is fitting

---

166. Krista Ophus, Prayer Update, February 18, 2017.

that we close with the last aspect of incarnational life being the final prayer Christ prayed for his disciples. His prayer was for the disciples and all the followers to come—that they would be one just as he and the Father are one. As has been true in reflecting the other practices of Christ in mission, the attention we give to the details of Christlike unity determines how clear or distorted the picture of Jesus will be to the world. A disunified church or ministry team gives a picture of Jesus robbed of its beauty like a bride unfit for marriage to the groom. A transformed church, however, full of the unity of the Spirit, expressed in Calvary love is a radiant picture of Christ to the city. Let's capture his image yet again as we pray along with Jesus, "Make us one, just as the Father and Jesus are one."

Capture His Image

As you have looked at Christ's prayer from John 17, if you are anything like me, you may have found your mind drifting a bit. You know these things are true. You know that Christ prayed for unity and has shown us the perfect example of relationship with the Father, but it may feel to you like you are trying to shoot an arrow at a quickly moving target. Perhaps you are in a situation so rattled by discord, arrogance, and brokenness that the words of Jesus seem so far away right now. Pause. Think about to whom Jesus spoke these words. He prays this prayer loud enough for disciples to hear him—most of whom deny him as he goes to the cross. Still, he prays entrusting the Spirit to do his work.

Perhaps the lesson for us is to not fixate on how far we must go or what mess is sitting in our laps right now. Let us gaze once more on the resurrected Christ: victorious, triumphant, and committed in love to you. Committed in love to your family, to your church, and to your community. Fix your gaze there as you remember the call of Jesus in unity. Let's focus on God's dream for your neighborhood.

If Jesus were sitting with you and your community leaders, what would he applaud in terms of your unity? What is going well?

In what ways are you unified with your family? Give specific examples.

How has your church and mission organization displayed Christlike unity in the last twelve months? Give specific examples.

How can you respond after realizing that one of Jesus' last prayers on earth was for you and your church? Where do you go in your mind and heart as you hear that?

The truth is out, and we cannot pretend to unknow what we know. What we know is that the body of Christ is divided in just about every possible way it could be divided. It's likely your neighborhood has ripple effects of those greater divisions. The stories from this chapter are probably not too far off from some of the situations you find yourself in on a regular basis. Discussing this topic will take some risk amongst those on your ministry team, and for those in key leadership positions it will require a listening ear. My prayer for those entering the next set of questions is that the Spirit will allow each person to lower his defenses in order that the Spirit would do his work. Let's start the unity prayer as we discuss.

Where do you feel tension in your family when it comes to unity? What are some practical next steps as you move forward?

In your local ministry or local church, what are the most present struggles when it comes to unity? Where are you not being heard? How are you not listening? What are some practical next steps?

As you read back over the prayer from John 17, what stands out to you after identifying the current tensions within your family or ministry/church?

How could your church or ministry be a catalyst in bringing unity to the broader neighborhood?

Pray the John 17 prayer together. Have each person pray one line at a time, and pray this prayer over the specific issues just raised.

Unity and walking in love are the evidences to our neighbors and cities that Jesus is alive. That is a pretty potent realization and calls the bluff on any superficial, glossed-over Christian ministry that we portray. We know the truth, our neighbors probably have already identified the weakness, and most importantly Christ knows the full score. Despite all of this, the prayer of Jesus still rings true, and the Holy Spirit is calling us towards unity. We can either face the truth with grace or turn from it and hide. The path ahead is straightforward really.

The hope of the world is Jesus, and that hope is evident through those in our cities humbly walking together in love. May the love of Jesus who gave himself away be the same love that is in our churches and ministry teams. May the unity that Christ had with his Father be echoed in our lives as we walk over the mountaintops and into the valleys. Jesus made no mistake when he called us to the city, and his undying love and mission for us is unmoved. Perhaps there is no more fitting way to close the chapter than to slow down and pray the unity prayer of Jesus once more line by line.

My prayer is not for them alone. I pray also for those who will believe in me through their message,

> *that all of them may be one, Father, just as you are in me and I am in you.*
> *May they also be in us so that the world may believe that you have sent me.*
> *I have given them the glory that you gave me, that they may be one as we are one—I in them and you in me—so that they may be brought to complete unity.*
> *Then the world will know that you sent me and have loved them even as you have loved me (John 17:20-23).*

Conclusion

Our Father in heaven,
hallowed be your name,
your kingdom come,
your will be done,
on earth as it is in heaven. (Matt. 6:9-10)

Jesus came to earth in the most humble, unlikely way imaginable and lived a perfect, awesome life. His life was one of sacrifice, surrender, and love. For 2,000 years the cities of this world have been captivated with him. Institutions have come and gone, structures have risen and fallen, liturgies have phased in and phased out. But Jesus in all his beauty cannot be shaken. He is just as compelling as he has ever been, and he finds himself walking through some of the most neglected neighborhoods of our world. He is alive. He is at work. He invites us afresh to reflect his image in the city.

The Bhutanese-Nepali in Pittsburgh and Minneapolis-St. Paul, the Hispanic communities of Chicago and Fresno, and so many places in between show us in flesh and blood that the Spirit's work is not done. From the explosive growth in the church in ethnic America to the most difficult circumstances in our neighborhoods, we see a task unfinished. There are more parties to be attended, more prayers to be offered, more sacrifices to be given, more disciples to be made. Perhaps more than ever, today is our Gethsemane. We know there is a long fight ahead, and the mission before us will require complete surrender to our Master Servant, Jesus.

In Acts 1, Jesus sat eyeball to eyeball with the disciples, and he left them with a promise. He promised that the Holy Spirit would come and empower them to do his work as they would be witnesses throughout the cities and towns of the globe. We too have not been left alone to struggle conjuring up grit and grind to make this all happen. The Holy Spirit is with us and that Spirit is being demonstrated in great power. The Spirit is enabling so many in the urban context to reflect Jesus. In mission. In prayer. In suffering. In discipleship. In compassion. In humility. In family. In justice. In community. And in unity. He is with us.

I hope that you have had a chance to slowly work through *Reflecting Jesus in the City* and that you and your ministry team have reached a place of renewed commitment to Christlike life and mission. Capturing and reflecting the clear image of Christ in your community is the most challenging, rewarding, and Christ-exalting journey you will ever take. In the days and weeks ahead may we echo the prayer of Jesus for the hallowing of God's name. In every corner of our neighborhoods may his name be hallowed. May his Kingdom come. May his will be done in the city as it is in heaven.

Bibliography

Amador, Paco. "Christianity's Most Vivid Celebration is a Meal." *Christianity Today*. March 2, 2017. Accessed March 14, 2017. http://www.christianitytoday.com/edstetzer/2017/february/christianitys-most-vivid-celebration-is-meal.html.

—. "Urban Issues in Ministry." Presentation, International Teams US Area Leaders, Elgin, Illinois. May 2-6, 2015.

Babbel, Susanne. "Compassion Fatigue." *Psychology Today*. July 4, 2012. Accessed February 8, 2017. https://www.psychologytoday.com/blog/somatic-psychology/201207/compassion-fatigue.

Bailey, Kenneth. *Jesus Through Middle Eastern Eyes*. Downers Grove, IL: IVP, 2007.

Bakke, Raymond. *A Theology as Big as the City*. Downers Grove, IL: IVP, 1997.

—. *The Urban Christian*. Downers Grove, IL: InterVarsity Press, 1987.

Beck, Richard. "Repent, The Kingdom of Heaven is at Hand: A Lenten Reflection." *Experimental Theology*. March 24, 2014. Accessed January 26, 2017. http://experimentaltheology.blogspot.com/2014/03/repent-kingdom-of-heaven-is-at-hand.html.

Benesh, Sean. *View from the Urban Loft: Developing a Theological Framework for Understanding the City*. Eugene, OR: Wipf and Stock Publishers, 2011.

Bethel Christian Fellowship. "About Us, Our Calling." n.d. Accessed March 23, 2017. http://betheltwincities.org/who-we-are/our-calling.

Bista, Dor Bahadur. *Fatalism in Development: Nepal's Struggle for Modernization*. Calcutta: Orient Longman, 1991.

Blomberg, Craig L. *The New American Commentary*. Vol. 2, *Matthew*. Holman, 1992.

Bock, Darrell. *Luke: The NIV Application Commentary From Biblical Text to Contemporary Life*. ePub ed. Grand Rapids, MI: Zondervan, 2014.

Boyd, Gregory. *God at War: The Bible and Spiritual Conflict*. Rev. ed. Downers Grove, IL: IVP, 2014.

—. *The Myth of a Christian Nation: How the Quest for Political Power is Destroying the Church*. Grand Rapids, MI: Zondervan, 2005.

Boyle, Gregory. *Tattoos on the Heart: The Power of Boundless Compassion*. New York: Free Press, 2010.

Brandt, Molly. "Bhutanese-Nepali Story." Poetic Project Presentation for *Introduction to the Arts*. Colorado Christian University, Lakewood, CO, December 12, 2016.

Breen, Mike. *Building a Discipling Culture*. Pawleys Islands, SC: 3 Dimension Ministries, 2011.

Brooks, Jonathan. "I'm Here Because You're Here." In *Making Neighborhoods Whole*, by Wayne Gordon and John Perkins, 64-70. Downers Grove, IL: IVP, 2013.

Brown, Brenton. "Humble King." Vineyard UK: 1999.

Brueggemann, Walter. *Hopeful Imagination: Prophetic Voices in Exile*. Minneapolis, MN: Fortress Press, 1986.

Bruno, Christopher R. "Jesus is Our Jubilee." *Journal of Evangelical Theological Studies*, JETS 53:1 (March 2010): 81-101.

Byrd, Michael F. *Evangelical Theology: A Biblical and Systematic Introduction*. Grand Rapids, MI: Zondervan, 2013.

Carlson, Ken. *Effective English Ministry: Reaching the Next Generation in Ethnic Immigrant Churches*. Kenneth Carlson, Self-Published, 2015.

Carr, Dhyanchand. "Jesus' Identification with Galilee and Dalit Hermeneutic," n.d. Accessed February 9, 2017. http://cca.org.hk/home/ctc/ctc03-03/ctc03-03b.htm .

Carson, D.A. *Love in Hard Places*. Wheaton, IL: Crossway Books, 2002.

—."*The Supremacy of Christ and Love in a Postmodern World*." Message, Desiring God 2006 National Conference. September 30, 2006. Accessed March 21, 2017. http://www.desiringgod.org/messages/the-supremacy-of-christ-and-love-in-a-postmodern-world

Carteret, Marcia. "Culture and Family Dynamics." *Dimensions of Culture*. November 2010. Accessed February 23, 2017. http://www.dimensionsofculture.com/2010/11/culture-and-family-dynamics/.

Castillo, Andrea, Barbara Anderson, and Bonhia Lee. "Apartments crawling with mice, roaches, but fearful tenants stay quiet." *McClatchy DC*

Bureau. May 8, 2016. Accessed March 3, 2017.
http://www.mcclatchydc.com/news/nation-
world/national/mcclatchys-america/article76429037.html.

Caufey, John. "To Release the Oppressed: Reclaiming a Biblical Theology of Liberation." *Jubilee Center.* n.d. Accessed November 23, 2016.
http://www.jubilee-centre.org/to-release-the-oppressed-reclaiming-
a-biblical-theology-of-liberation-by-john-coffey/.

Cleveland, Christena. *Disunity in Christ: Uncovering the Hidden Forces That Keep Us Apart.* Downers Grove, IL: IVP, 2013.

Cloud, Henry and John Townsend. *Boundaries: When to Say Yes, How to Say No.* Grand Rapids, MI: Zondervan, 2008.

Conn, Harvie M., and Manuel Ortiz. *Urban Ministry: The Kingdom, the City, and the People of God.* Downers Grove, IL: IVP, 2001.

Cramer, Dan. "Mission in Smaller Churches." *Catalyst Services.* October 2014. Accessed February 10, 2017. http://catalystservices.org/wp-
content/uploads/2014/10/Missions-in-Smaller-Churches.pdf.

Creps, Earl. "Finding Your Prophetic Voice." Lecture, Assemblies of God Theological Seminary Chapel, Springfield, MO, 2006.

Dau, John Bul, and Michael S. Sweeney. *God Grew Tired of Us.* Washington D.C.: National Geographic Society, 2007.

Davies, Guy. "Cicero on the Offense of the Cross." *Exiled Preacher, Displaced Fragments: Theology, Ministry Interviews, and Reviews.* March 12, 2012. Accessed December 30, 2016.
http://exiledpreacher.blogspot.com/2012/03/cicero-on-offence-of-
cross.html.

DeYoung, Kevin. "Jesus, Friend of Sinners, But How?" *The Gospel Coalition.* March 4, 2014. Accessed March 14, 2017.
https://blogs.thegospelcoalition.org/kevindeyoung/2014/03/04/jesu
s-friend-of-sinners-but-how/.

Elmer, Duane. *Cross-Cultural Servanthood: Serving the World in Christlike Humility.* Downers Grove, IL: IVP, 2006.

Emerson, Michael O. and Christian Smith. *Divided By Faith: Evangelical Religion and the Problem of Race in America.* New York: Oxford University Press, 2000.

Ferdinando, Keith. "Jesus the Theological Educator." *Themelious Vol. 38 No. 3*. November 2013. Accessed January 26, 2017. http://themelios.thegospelcoalition.org/article/jesus-the-theological-educator.

Fung, Patrick. "Live to be Forgotten Interview." *Urbana Missions Conference 2006*. Accessed February 9, 2017. https://vimeo.com/8433862?lite=1.

Fujino, Gary, Timothy R. Sisk, and Tereso C. Casiño, ed. *Reaching the City: Reflections on Urban Mission for the Twenty-First Century*. Evangelical Missiological Society 20. Pasadena, CA: William Carey Library, 2012.

Fuqua, Andy. "The Other Side." *Engineering the Church for Kingdom Glimpses*. July 13, 2015. Accessed December 23, 2016. http://www.andyfuqua.com/2015/07/13/the-other-side/.

Gardner, Marilyn R. *Between Worlds: Essays on Culture and Belonging*. Doorlight Publications, 2014.

Gine, Pratap C., and Jacob Cherian, "John" in *South Asia Bible Commentary*, edited by Brian Wintle. Grand Rapids, MI: Zondervan, 2015.

Gurnall, William. *The Christian in Complete Armour*. Vol. 2. Lindale, Texas: World Challenge Inc., 1988.

Gordon, Wayne, and John Perkins. *Making Neighborhoods Whole*. Downers Grove, IL: IVP, 2013.

Gordon, Wayne. *Who is My Neighbor?: Lessons Learned from a Man Left for Dead*. Grand Rapids, MI: Baker Books, 2010.

Gutierrez, Gustavo. *A Theology of Liberation*. Rev. ed. Maryknoll, NY: Orbis, 2012.

Gwaltney, Darrell. "Good News for the Poor (Luke 4:18)." *Bible Commentary for the New Baptist Covenant,* August 16, 2007. Accessed November 25, 2016. http://www.ethicsdaily.com/good-news-for-the-poor-luke-4-18-bible-commentary-for-the-new-baptist-covenant-cms-9316.

Hansen, G. Walter. "The Emotions of Jesus." *Christianity Today*. February 3, 1997. Accessed February 10, 2017. http://www.christianitytoday.com/ct/1997/february3/7t2042.html.

Harold, Phillip. "You Can't Choose Your Friends." *Patheos Evangelical*. October 11, 2013. Accessed February 23, 2017.

http://www.patheos.com/blogs/fareforward/2013/10/you-cant-choose-your-friends/.

Heuertz, Christopher L., and Christine D. Pohl. *Friendship at the Margins: Discovering Mutuality in Service and Mission.* Downers Grove, IL: InterVarsity Press, 2010.

Hiebert, Paul G., and Eloise Hiebert Meneses. *Incarnational Ministry: Planting Churches in Band, Tribal, Peasant and Urban Societies.* Grand Rapids, MI: Baker Academic, 1995.

Huckins, John. "Worshipping the Idol of Safety." *Sojourners.* March 23, 2016. Accessed February 24, 2017. https://sojo.net/articles/worshiping-idol-safety.

Jackson, Wayne. "The Compassion of Christ." *Christian Courier.* n.d. Accessed February 10, 2017. https://www.christiancourier.com/articles/947-compassion-of-christ-.

Jenkins, Dave. "The Work and Person of the Holy Spirit in the Gospel of John." *Blue Letter Bible.* March 5, 2013. Accessed March 22, 2017. http://blogs.blueletterbible.org/blb/2013/03/05/the-work-and-person-of-the-holy-spirit-in-the-gospel-of-john/.

"Kenan Institute of Ethics at Duke University." *Introduction to Bhutanese Refugees in Nepal.* 2013. Accessed April 20, 2017. http://kenan.ethics.duke.edu/uprooted-rerouted/introductions/nepal.html.

Keener, Craig. *The IVP Bible Background Commentary: New Testament.* Downers Grove, IL: InterVarsity Academic, 1993.

Keller, Timothy. *Generous Justice: How God's Grace Makes Us Just.* New York, NY: Penguin Books, 2010.

—. *Loving the City: Doing Gospel-Centered Ministry in Your City.* Grand Rapids, MI: Zondervan Publishing, 2016.

—. *Ministries of Mercy: The Call of the Jericho Road.* 2nd ed. Phillipsburg, NJ: P&R Publishing, 1997.

—. *Walking with God Through Pain and Suffering.* New York, NY: Penguin Books, 2013.

Kierkegaard, Soren. *The Concept of Anxiety.* Edited and Translated by Alastair Hannay. New York, NY: Liveright Publishing, 2014.

Knott, Kim. *Hinduism: A Very Short Introduction*. Oxford: Oxford University Press, 1998.

Koech, Joseph. "The Spirit Motif in Luke 4:14-30, Acts 1:8, and the Church Today." Africa *Journal of Evangelical Theology* 27, no. 2 (2008).

Kraybill, Donald. *The Upside-Down Kingdom*. Rev. ed. Harrisonburg, VA: Herald Press, 2012.

Ladd, George Eldon. *The Gospel of the Kingdom*. 1959. Reprint, Paternoster Press, 2000.

Langmead, Ross. *Word Made Flesh: Towards an Incarnational Missiology (American Society of Missiology Dissertation Series)*. UPA, 2004.

LaVerdiere, Eugene. "Dining in the Kingdom of God." Archdiocese of Chicago: Liturgy Training Publication, 1994.

Lavine, Amy. *Short Stories by Jesus: The Enigmatic Parables of a Controversial Rabbi*. New York, NY: HarperCollins, 2014.

Lee, Erica. *The Making of Asian America: A History*. New York: Simon and Schuster, 2015.

Lee, Helen. "Chapter 4: Healthy Leaders, Healthy Households." In *Growing Healthy Asian-American Churches,* edited by Peter Cha, Steve Kang, and Helen Lee. Downers Grove, IL: IVP, 2006.

Lewis, C.S. *A Grief Observed: Collective Letters of C.S. Lewis*. 1961. Reprint, HarperCollins, 1996.

Lim, Bo. "A Return to Justice and Righteousness." *Seattle Pacific University Lectio*. n.d. Accessed March 1, 2017. http://blog.spu.edu/lectio/a-return-to-justice-and-righteousness/.

Lingenfelter, Sherwood G., and Marvin K Mayers. *Ministering Cross-Culturally: An Incarnational Model for Personal Relationships*. Grand Rapids, MI: Baker Academic, 1986.

Lupton, Robert. *Theirs is the Kingdom: Celebrating the Gospel in Urban America*. New York: HarperCollins, 2010.

Marinella, Mark A. *Died He for Me: A Physician's View of the Crucifixion of Jesus Christ*. 2008. Reprint, Nordskog Publishing, 2016.

McCarthy, Kristin. "Adaptation of Immigrant Children to the United States: A Review of the Literature." Working Paper #98-03. Center for Research on Child Well-Being. March 1998. Accessed February 23,

2017 http://crcw.princeton.edu/workingpapers/WP98-03-McCarthy.pdf.

McKnight, Scott, N.T. Wright, and Dallas Willard. *The King Jesus Gospel: The Original Good News Revisited*. Rev. ed. Grand Rapids, MI: Zondervan, 2016.

Mohan, Joe. "Church in Nepal is Growing Rapidly." *Calvin Chimes*. March 12, 2014. Accessed December 1, 2016. http://www.calvin.edu/chimes/2014/03/12/church-in-nepal-is-growing-rapidly/.

Morgan, Christopher W., and Robert A. Peterson, ed. *The Kingdom of God*. Wheaton, IL: Crossway Books, 2012.

Myers, Bryant L. *Walking with the Poor: Principles and Practices of Transformational Development*. Rev. ed. Maryknoll, NY: Orbis Books, 2011.

Neill, Stephen. *Creative Tensions*. Edinborough: London Press, 1959.

Nickeas, Peter, E. Jason Wambgsans, and Mary Schmich. "Benny and Jorge and the Quest for Peace in Little Village." *Chicago Tribune*. May 1, 2017. Accessed June 1, 2017. http://www.chicagotribune.com/news/peacemakers/ct-little-village-met-20170421-story.html.

Nouwen, Henri, Donald McNeill, and Douglas Morrison. *Compassion: A Reflection on the Christian Life*. Rev. ed. Image Publishers, 2006.

Nouwen, Henri. "Solitude, Ministry, and Community." *Leadership Journal*, 1995.

Osiek, Carolyn. "Jesus and Cultural Values: Family Life as an Example." Paper presented at the Images of Jesus Seminar, Research Institute for Theology and Religion, University of South Africa, September 3-4, 1997.

Parnell, Jonathan. "Jesus Turns the Tables." *Desiring God*. March 30, 2015. Accessed February 28, 2017. http://www.desiringgod.org/articles/jesus-turns-the-tables.

—. "One Way to Glory in the Cross." *Desiring God*. November 28, 2011. Accessed March 21, 2017. http://www.desiringgod.org/articles/one-way-to-glory-in-the-cross.

Pearson, Barbara Zurer. *Raising a Bilingual Child*. Living Language, 2008.

Perkins, Harvey. "Four Bible Studies on Development in the Asian Context."
     South East Journal of Asian Theology, No. 21, 1980: 79-80.

Perkins, John M. *Beyond Charity: The Call to Christian Community
     Development*. Grand Rapids, MI: Baker Books, 1993.

—. *With Justice for All: A Strategy for Community Development*. Rev. ed.
     Grand Rapids, MI: Baker Books, 2011.

Persyn, Johan. "The Embarrassment of Crucifixion." February 22, 2017.
     Accessed February 23, 2017.
     http://www.johanpersyn.com/embarrassment-crucifixion/.

"The Physical Death of Jesus Christ: Study of the Mayo Clinic." *Journal of the
     American Medical Association*. 1986. Accessed December 29, 2016.
     http://www.frugalsites.net/jesus/crucifixion.htm.

Piper, John. *God is the Gospel: Meditations on God's Love as the Gift of
     Himself*. Wheaton, IL: Crossway Books, 2005.

—. *When I Don't Desire God: How to Fight for Joy*. Wheaton, IL: Crossway
     Books, 2004.

Pohl, Christine. *Living Into Community: Cultivating Practices That Sustain
     Us*. Grand Rapids, MI: Eerdmans Publishing, 2011.

—. *Making Room: Rediscovering Hospitality as a Christian Tradition*.
     Grand Rapids, MI: Eerdmans Publishing, 1999.

Pollock, David C., and Ruth E. Van Reken. *Third Culture Kids: Growing Up
     Among Worlds*. Rev. ed. Boston: Nicholas Brealey Publishing, 2009.

Priess, Danielle. "Why Nepal Has One of the Fastest-Growing Christian
     Populations." *NPR: Stories of Life in a Changing World*. February 3,
     2016. Accessed November 24, 2016.
     http://www.npr.org/sections/goatsandsoda/2016/02/03/463965924
     /why-nepal-has-one-of-the-worlds-fastest-growing-christian-
     populations.

Rah, Soong-Chan. *The Next Evangelicalism: Freeing the Church From
     Western Cultural Captivity*. Downers Grove, IL: IVP, 2009.

—. *Prophetic Lament: A Call for Justice in Troubled Times*. Downers Grove,
     IL: IVP, 2015.

Randle, Drew. "How Should We Respond to Betrayal." *Christianity Today:
     Christian Bible Studies*. 2013. Accessed December 29, 2016.

http://www.christianitytoday.com/biblestudies/bible-answers/spirituallife/how-should-we-respond-to-betrayal.html.

Ransleben, Kim. "The Biggest Barrier for Students Going to the Mission Field." *Desiring God.* January 15, 2015. Accessed February 22, 2017. http://www.desiringgod.org/articles/the-biggest-barrier-to-students-going-to-the-mission-field.

Reinke, Tony. "10 Questions on Prayer with Tim Keller." *Desiring God: Gospel Coalition.* October 31, 2014. Accessed December 24, 2016. http://www.desiringgod.org/articles/10-questions-on-prayer-with-tim-keller.

"Retinitis Pigmentosa." *Foundation Fighting Blindness.* n.d. Accessed December 29, 2016. http://www.blindness.org/retinitis-pigmentosa.

Robinson, Erick. "How Support-raising Keeps Parachurch Ministries White." *Minister Different: Pursuing Justice in Support-raising.* n.d. Accessed March 21, 2017. http://ministerdifferent.com/support-raising-white/.

Roenigk, Emily. "5 Reasons 'Poverty Porn' Empowers the Wrong Person." *Huffington Post.* April 16, 2014. Accessed December 28, 2016. http://www.huffingtonpost.com/emily-roenigk/poverty-charity-media_b_5155627.html.

Rohane, Kyle. "Are Pastors Discarding the Evangelical Label? *Christianity Today.*   November 2016. Accessed March 19, 2017. http://www.christianitytoday.com/pastors/2016/november-web-exclusives/are-evangelical-pastors-discarding-evangelical-label.html.

Russell, Walt. "The Anointing with the Holy Spirit in Luke-Acts." *Trinity Journal 202,* (1986): 52.

Sinclair, Daniel. *A Vision of the Possible: Pioneer Church Planting in Teams.* Waynesboro, GA: Authentic, 2006.

Smith, T. Aaron. *Thriving in the City: A Guide for Sustainable Incarnational Ministry Among the Urban Poor.* Pomona, CA: Servant Partners Press, 2015.

Snyder, Howard A. *The Community of the King.* Downers Grove, IL: IVP Academic, 2004.

Solano, Claude. "Urban Ministry: A Study in Contextual Ministry." Doctor of Ministry diss., *Asbury Theological Seminary,* 2011.

Sproul, R.C. *Does Prayer Change Things?* Sanford, FL: Reformation Trust
Publishers, 2009.

St. Paul Public Schools Office of Multilingual Learning. "SPPS EL Facts." n.d.
Accessed March 23, 2017.
http://spps.schoolwires.net/Domain/10453.

Stein, Robert. *Mark: Baker Exegetical Commentary on the New Testament.*
Grand Rapids, MI: Baker Academic, 2008.

Strega, Susan. "The View from Post-structural Margins: Epistemology and
Methodology." In *Research as Resistance: Critical, Indigenous, and
Anti-Oppressive,* edited by Leslie Brown and Susan Strega. Toronto:
Canadian Scholars' Press, 2005.

Stronstad, Roger. "The Holy Spirit in Luke-Acts." *Paraclete 23*, no. 2 (Spring
1989): 20-22.

Takatemjen. "Luke." In *South Asia Bible Commentary.* Grand Rapids, MI:
Zondervan Publishing, 2015.

Teresa, Mother. "In the Heart of the World." n.d. Accessed December 3, 2016.
http://www.newworldlibrary.com/NewWorldLibraryUnshelved/tabi
d/767/articleType/ArticleView/articleId/19/Mother-Teresa-on-
Silence.aspx.

Tiede, David. "Proclaiming the Righteous Reign of Jesus: Luke 4 and the
Justice of God." *Word and World, Texts in Context* (Luther
Northwestern Theological Seminary). July 1, 1987.

Tiersma Watson, Jude. "Journey from Obedience to Joy." *Global Missiology*
(Oct. 2012).

Tiersma Watson, Jude. "What does it mean to be incarnational when we are
not the Messiah?" In *God So Loves the City*, rev. ed. by Charles Van
Engen and Jude Tiersma Watson. Eugene, OR: Wipf and Stock, 2009.

Tolan, Casey. "A Mysterious Mental Health Disorder is Afflicting Bhutanese
Refugees in America." *Fusion Magazine.* June 6, 2016. Accessed
November 23, 2016. http://fusion.net/story/310750/bhutan-
refugees-pittsburgh-mental-health/.

Tuff, Eve. "Suspending Damage: A Letter to Communities." *Harvard
Educational Review 79*, no. 3 (Fall 2009).

Urban Life Skills. n.d. Accessed April 30, 2017.
https://newlifecenters.org/our-programs/urban-life-skills/.

Van Engen, Charles, and Jude Tiersma. *God So Loves the City: Seeking a Theology of Urban Mission*. Rev. ed. Eugene, OR: Wipf and Stock, 2009.

Wan, Enoch. *Diaspora Missiology: Theory, Methodology, and Practice*. Portland, OR: Institute of Diaspora Studies, Western Seminary, 2011.

Watters, David. *At the Foot of the Snows*. Seattle, WA: Engage Faith Press, 2011.

Westfall, Cynthia Long. "Family in the Gospels and Acts." In *Family in the Bible: Exploring Customs, Culture, and Context*. Edited by Richard S. Hess and M. Daniel Carroll R. Grand Rapids, MI: Baker Academic, 2003.

Whitacre, Rodney A. "Jesus Concludes His Time with His Disciples By Praying to His Father." *IVP New Testament Commentary Series: John*, edited by Grant R. Osborne, vol. 4. Downers Grove, IL: IVP Academic, 2010. Accessed March 20, 2017. https://www.biblegateway.com/resources/commentaries/IVP-NT/John/Jesus-Concludes-Time-Alone.

Whitney, Donald S. "The Gospel and the Discipline of Solitude." *LifeWay Christian Resources*. n.d. Accessed December 22, 2016. http://www.lifeway.com/Article/spiritual-disciplines-gospel-solitude-donald-whitney.

Williams, David T. *Kenosis of God*. iUniverse Publications, 2009.

Williams, Jenny. "Jenny Williams: Our Interruptions Are Our Work." *Faith and Leadership*. August 4, 2009. Accessed December 15, 2016. https://www.faithandleadership.com/jenny-williams-our-interruptions-are-our-work.

Williamson, Mabel. *Have We No Rights? A Frank Discussion of the "Rights of Missionaries*. Rev. ed. 2011.

Winter, Ralph D., and Bruce A. Koch. "Finishing the Task: The Unreached People Challenge." In *Perspectives on the World Christian Movement: A Reader, 3rd ed.*, by Ralph D. Winter. Pasadena, CA: William Carey Library Pub., 1974.

Wright, Christopher J.H. *The Mission of God*. Downers Grove, IL: InterVarsity Press, 2006.

Trotter

—. *The Mission of God's People: A Biblical Theology of the Church's Mission.* Edited by Jonathan Lunde. Grand Rapids, MI: Zondervan, 2010.

Wright, N.T. "The Lord's Prayer as Paradigm of Christian Prayer." In *Into God's Presence: Prayer in the New Testament,* by R.L. Longenecker, 132-54. Grand Rapids, MI: Eerdmans, 2001.

—. *John for Everyone: The New Testament for the People of God.* Louisville, KY: John Knox Press, 2004.

—. *Luke for Everyone: The New Testament for Everyone.* Louisville, KY: Westminster John Knox Press, 2004.

Yong, Amos. *The Bible, Disability, and the Church: A New Vision of the People of God.* Grand Rapids, MI: William B. Eerdmans Publishing Co., 2011.

—. *The Future of Evangelical Theology: Soundings from the Asian-American Diaspora.* Downers Grove, IL: InterVarsity Press, 2014.

Zion Christian Church. "Networking in Missions." Accessed April 17, 2017. http://zioncc.org/connection-points/networking-in-missions.

Author Bio

John Trotter is Catalyst of One Collective in Pittsburgh and pastor of Love Carrick, a multi-ethnic house church network in the Carrick neighborhood. Graduating with a MA in Intercultural Studies from Asia Pacific Theological Seminary, he has served cross-culturally for the last 16 years in South and Southeast Asia, Minneapolis-St. Paul, and Pittsburgh. He writes on the intersection of Christ, community, the church, and culture at www.trotterj.com. He lives with his wife Charity and son Amos in the Carrick community of Pittsburgh where the door to their place is always open.

CPSIA information can be obtained
at www.ICGtesting.com
Printed in the USA
FSHW011248210220
67392FS